Ex Libris

A Time of Peace, Season of Innocence

by

Clarence G. Oliver, Jr.

Limited Edition

No. 715 of 750

Clarence G. Oliver, Jr.

BETWEEN WARS
1945-1950

A TIME OF PEACE,
SEASON OF INNOCENCE

A PHOTOGRAPHIC HISTORY –

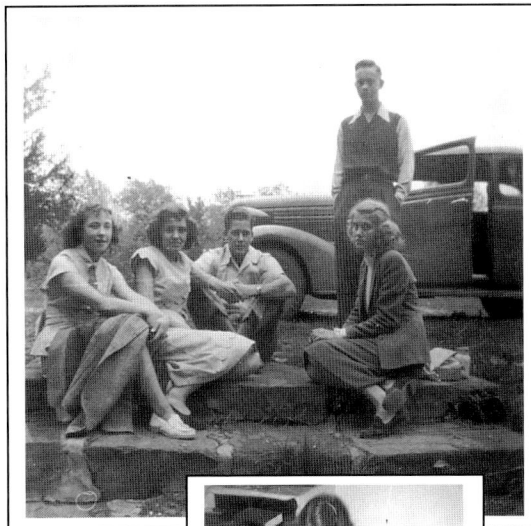

YOUNG PEOPLE IN A SMALL TOWN IN OKLAHOMA
BETWEEN WORLD WAR II AND THE KOREAN WAR

PHOTOGRAPHS AND TEXT
BY CLARENCE G. OLIVER, JR.

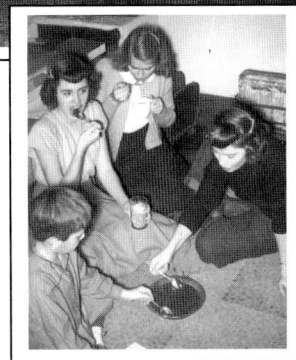

1

Between Wars
1945-1950

A TIME OF PEACE,
SEASON OF INNOCENCE

Young People in a Small Town in Oklahoma
Between World War II and The Korean War

✦

Clarence G. Oliver, Jr.

AuthorHouse
1663 Liberty Drive, Suite 200
Bloomington, IN 47403
888.519.5121
www.authorhouse.com

4

AuthorHouse ™
1663 Liberty Drive
Bloomington, IN 47403

© Copyright 2012, Clarence Grady Oliver, Jr. All rights reserved.

Published by AuthorHouse 5/25/2012

ISBN. 978-1-4634-1668-3 (dj)

Library of Congress Control Number: 2011908865

This book is printed on acid-free paper.

**Also By
Clarence G. Oliver, Jr.**

*Ethical Behavior
An Administrator's Guide:
Ethics and Values in School Administration*

*One from the Least
And Disappearing Generation:
A Memoir of a Depression-Era Kid*

*Tony Dufflebag
. . . and Other Remembrances
of the War in Korea*

Broken Arrow: The First Hundred Years
(Contributing Author and Co-Editor)

The History of Broken Arrow
(Storyline and Narration of Documentary DVD Movie)

A Time of Peace —

There is a time for everything and a season for every activity under heaven:
a time to be born and a time to die, a time to plant and a time to uproot,
a time to kill and a time to heal, a time to tear down and a time to build,
a time to weep and a time to laugh, a time to mourn and a time to dance,
a time to scatter stones and a time to gather them,
a time to embrace and a time to refrain,
a time to search and a time to give up,
a time to keep and a time to throw away,
a time to tear and a time to mend, a time to be silent and a time to speak,
a time to love and a time to hate, a time for war and a time for peace.

— Ecclesiastes 3:1-8

Innocence —

"They that know no evil will suspect none."

— *Ben Jonson*

Innocence most likely is in the "eye of the beholder." There is a thin line between being innocent and being naïve. Although the word can mean being not guilty of a particular wrongdoing, more generally, innocence is a state of unknowing, where youth and inexperience causes one to have an optimistic view of the world, a lack of wrongdoing, a lack of worldliness or sophistication. Innocence may decrease with age, but some of the beliefs and emotions remain as an influence in one's life.

—In Memory of—
Vinita June (Shirley) Oliver
1930-2009
my wife, my love, my best friend

—Dedication—
to our children,
Paul, Mark, Shirley
and their spouses;

to their children and their children's children,
to all the family—present and future—
that all may know what life was like
during a brief time of
"Peace" and "Innocence"

Contents —

10

Prologue —

The Beginning —

A childhood interest in photography led a young Clarence Oliver to dream of a career as a journalist-photographer. He devoted spare time to reading about photography in books and magazines found in the Ada City Library and practiced those self-taught skills using the family's old folding-bellows camera. Immediately after graduating from high school, one of the city's finest photographers offered him the opportunity to study the "art and science" of photography as an apprentice. He eagerly accepted. The pay would be minimal—just $7 per week. The real benefit, though, was the opportunity to learn through one-on-one instruction from a master photographer.

James Stansel, with training in the New York Institute of Photography and years of experience in portrait and commercial photography, owned and operated a Main Street studio that specialized in portrait and commercial photography, as well as wedding photography and other group projects. His work was of exceptional quality, reflecting his superior training and extensive experience. Those years as an apprentice to a master craftsman were followed by college preparation in journalism; work in a university photography department under the tutelage of another master photographer, and a brief stint as a free-lance photographer during the summer before the start of the Korean War.

Because of that extensive training, looking for opportunities and taking candid photographs became second nature to Oliver. During the high school and college years of 1945 to 1950, between the end of World War II and the beginning of the Korean War, Oliver snapped hundreds of photographs of family and friends going about daily activities, events at school, church, community scenes and other activities. Some photographs were developed and printed. Many were never printed. Negatives of all the photographs were filed away in boxes. Encouraged by his family to tell the story of young people living in a small town during the years "between wars," Oliver retrieved the negatives and prints and selected some to share in this unusual photographic history of a short and very special "Time of Peace, Season of Innocence."

The Photographer —

Self Portrait —

Age 17 (1946)

Photo taken with a simple camera that did not have time delay shutter. A string was used to snap the shutter.

14

World War II Ends . . .
A Time of Peace Begins

The Stars and Stripes
August 15, 1945

Seattle Post-Intelligencer
August 15, 1945

Peace Came Slowly —

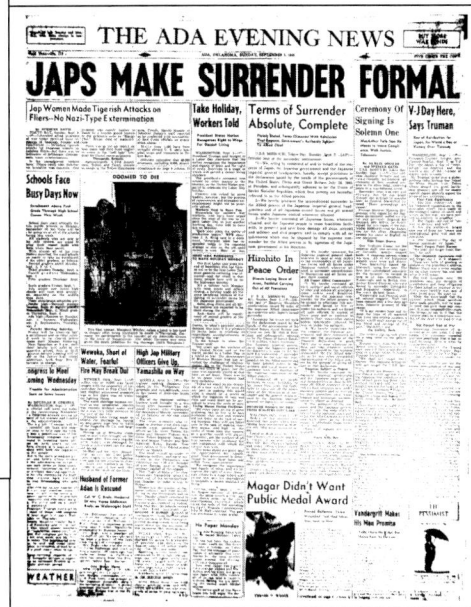

THE ADA EVENING NEWS

STUNNED ENEMY ADMITS BOMB DAMAGE

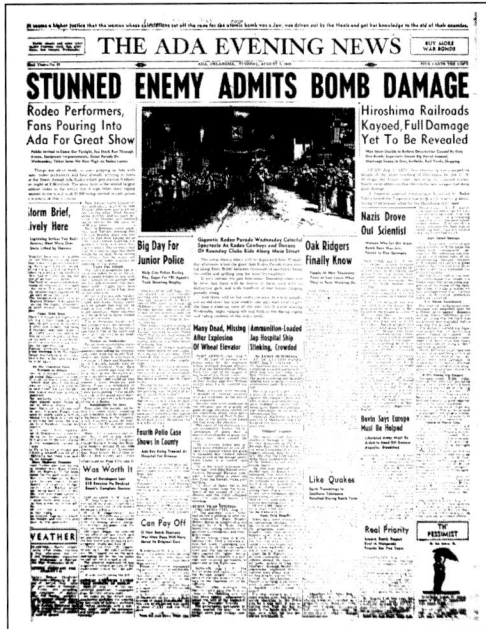

The Ada Evening News
August 7, 1945

THE ADA EVENING NEWS

JAPS MAKE SURRENDER FORMAL

The Ada Evening News
September 1, 1945

Used with permission from The Ada Evening News. © 1945. 2010. The News Publishing Company.

The Korean War Begins . . .
A Time of Peace Ends —

THE ADA EVENING NEWS — FINAL EDITION

U.S. TROOPS MOVE UP TOWARD BATTLE

Campaign Guns Roar In Final Drive; Big Rally Monday Night | **K. C. Police Figure Shot** | **On Way To Combat Area Near Suwon, S. Koreans Rally Again To Halt Drive**

Holiday Already In Effect For Some, Others Plan For July 4

Oil Activities At In-Between Stage On Several Area Wells

Crime Probers To Visit Four Cities In On. Spot Inquiries

THE ADA EVENING NEWS — HOME EDITION

City Soon to Advertise for Bids on Sewer

Kilroy Is Right Here—

N. Koreans Reach Outskirts Of Seoul, Defenses Collapse

Find Pieces of Plane And Human Flesh | **Four Planes Strafe Seoul** | **Truman Pledges U.S. Support Now for UN**

U.N. Sends Demand N. Korean Forces Withdraw Armies

Senate Probers Get Copy of Service-Jaffe Talk in 1945

Mrs. Troy Jones, Formerly of Ada, Dies at Chickasha

Negro Leader Hits At Taft and Lucas

Uncertainty, Some Worry Here Over Developments in Korea

Death Takes Four In Road Accident Over State Sunday

Low Spends Weeks Lost in Sink Hole

Louisiana Proved On Alligator Use

Collision Causes Beehive Activity

Rock Island Finds State Operations

W. Virginia Finds Floods Leave 21 Dead; 31 Missing

Man Sharpe Found In Hobbs, N. Mex.

Flying Saucers? They Know Plenty

Shudder of Apprehension Over War Possibilities Hits West

Weather—Hot

The Ada Evening News
July 2, 1950

The Ada Evening News
June 26, 1950

Used with permission from The Ada Evening News. © 1945. 2010. The News Publishing Company.

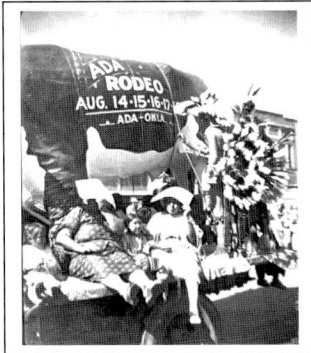

Chapter One

The Hometown —

18

Hometown Ada —

Ada's downtown in the mid 1940s was busy—especially on Saturdays. The McSwain Theater was the premier of five downtown movie theaters. The McSwain was Ada's first-run movie theater and very much the city's most popular entertainment center.

No new automobiles were produced again until after World War II ended. Most of the parked cars are 1941 or earlier models.

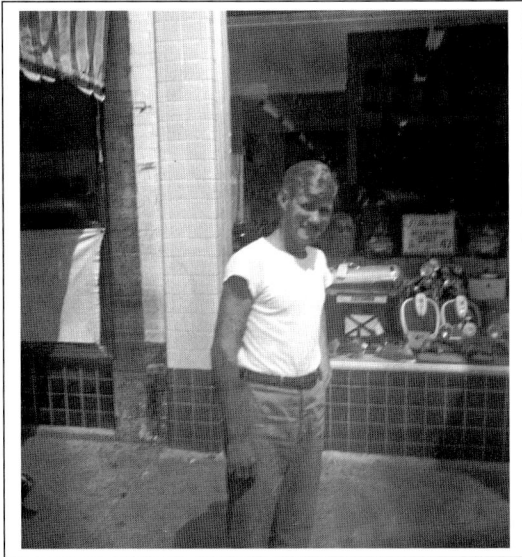

Main Street Scene
Ada, Oklahoma
— 1946

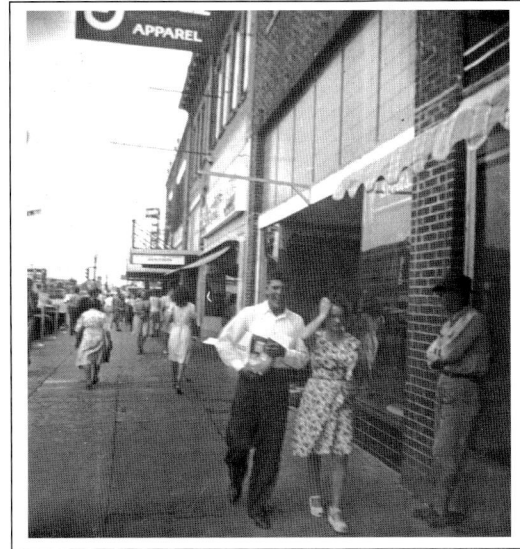

Strolling shoppers on East Main Street

20

City of Influence —

During the 1940s, Ada, Oklahoma, with a population approaching 20,000, was considered a city of influence in the region. The Chamber of Commerce promoted the city as one built on commerce, business, industry, oil and agriculture, as well as being a community of great churches, good schools and neighborly citizens.

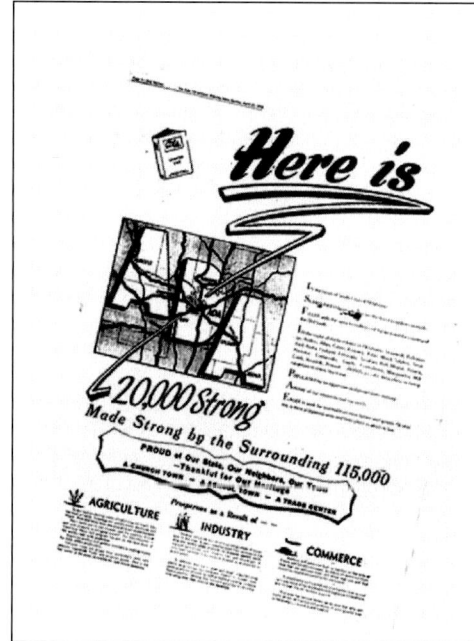

The Ada Evening News
— Sunday, April 25, 1948

Ada Rodeo History —

Rodeo is a sport that is deeply rooted in American history and is uniquely American. It is a sport that grew out of an industry—the cattle business in its early years.

From its beginnings in impromptu contests between cowboys at round-up time on the frontier ranches to today's mega events and PBR spectaculars, rodeo has evolved as an American institution. In no place is that more true than in small town Ada, Oklahoma. When the local firemen staged a rodeo in 1935, it was successful and became a yearly event. Many local supporters were involved and all profits were put back into the operation to improve facilities and increase the size of purses paid to the performers. This attracted not only local rodeo stars such as Dick Truitt and Everett Shaw, but also brought in the best rodeo performers, clowns and feature acts from all over the nation, many of whom returned year after year. In the 1940s, the Ada Firemen's Rodeo surpassed the great Cheyenne, Wyoming, rodeo in both attendance and size of purses.

Rodeo in Ada started in an informal manner in 1921 and resulted in a three-day "Big Ada Roundup and Frontier Days" event for June 16-18, 1921. There was talk of staging another, but that didn't happen. Then, in the summer of 1935, some off-duty Ada firemen and friends were sitting around talking about what might be done to brighten up a usually dull August time. And, the idea of staging a rodeo was proposed. Such an event was hastily organized, three weeks later, August 17-18, 1935, the Ada Firemen's Rodeo was held.

In the years that followed, the Ada Rodeo became a significant event that attracted international attention. The Ada Rodeo of 1945, with attendance estimated at more than 50,000, set a record. By 1946, the Ada Rodeo was billed as the "second largest outdoor rodeo in the world." Then, in 1948, the Ada Rodeo surpassed the Cheyenne, Wyoming, Rodeo in attendance and prize money, and for that year, was the largest outdoor rodeo in the world. (Klepper 2009).

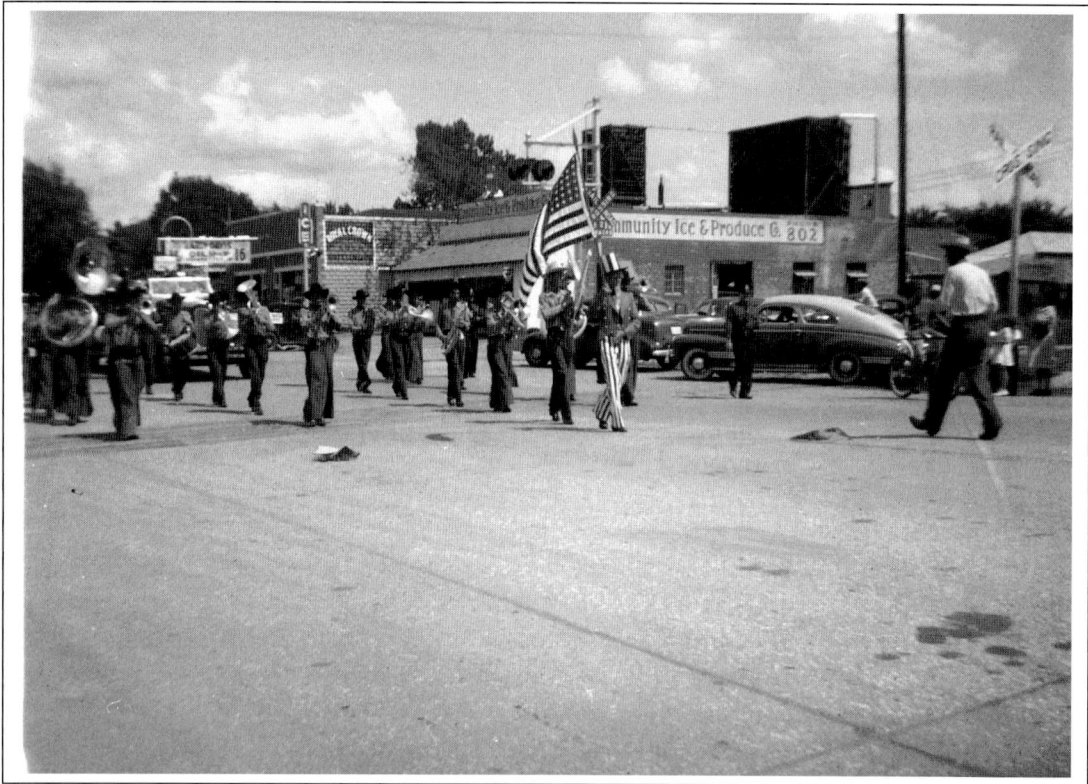

Oklahoma State Prison Cowboy Marching Band
Ada Firemen's International Rodeo Parade — August 1948

The Ada Rodeo was "Big News." Full page advertisements and Page One banner headlines promoted the event that by 1948 had surpassed the Cheyenne, Wyoming, Rodeo in attendance and prize money, and for that year, was the largest outdoor rodeo in the world.

The Ada Evening News
— Sunday, August 8, 1948

The Ada Evening News
— Tuesday, August 9, 1949

Kiowa Indians —

Kiowa Indian ceremonial dancers frequently participated in the Ada Rodeo. In addition to marching and performing along the parade route, a large delegation of ceremonial dancers from the Kiowa Indian tribe of southwestern Oklahoma, dressed in elaborate ceremonial costumes, also performed ceremonial dances following the "grand entry" of roundup clubs and other entertainment for opening night of the resurging rodeo in 1944.

During the 1948 Ada Rodeo Parade, young Kiowa Indian dancers entertained spectators along the parade route as they performed on a float, riding with the famous bull, "Ferninand."

Rodeo Parade —

Kiowa Indian dancers were popular performers during many Rodeos. Squaws "endure the sun" while a young dancer entertains parade viewers.

Young couple with a classic buggy.

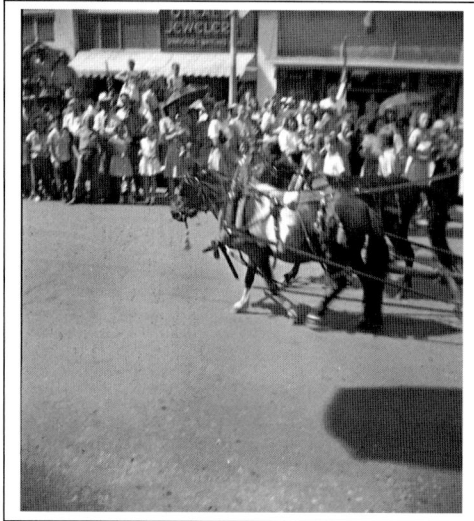

Round Up clubs from throughout the state, and some from other states, entertained parade viewers with hundreds of horses and riders.

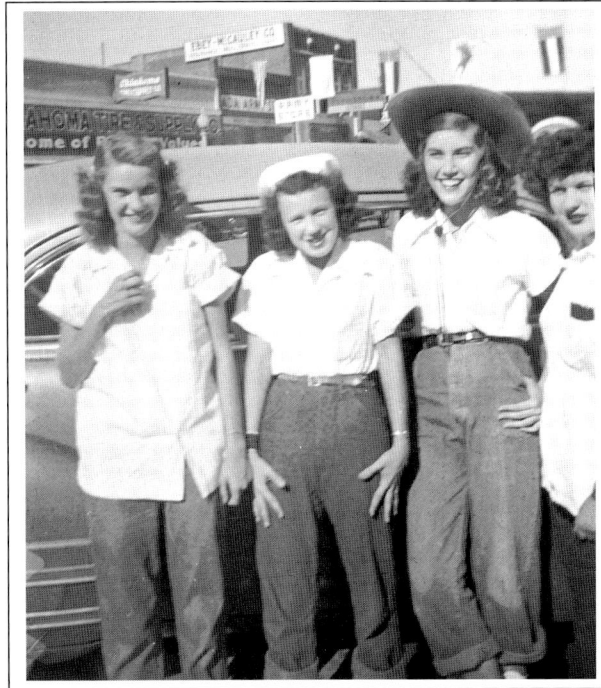

Young Ladies at the Parade —

In 1948, the Ada Rodeo replaced the Cheyenne, Wyoming, Frontier Days as "Number One" among rodeos. A crowd estimated at 7,000 jammed downtown Ada's Main Street to watch the parade pass.

A total of 25 roundup clubs and 18 floats appeared. By actual count, there were 1,082 horses in the parade that year—setting another record.

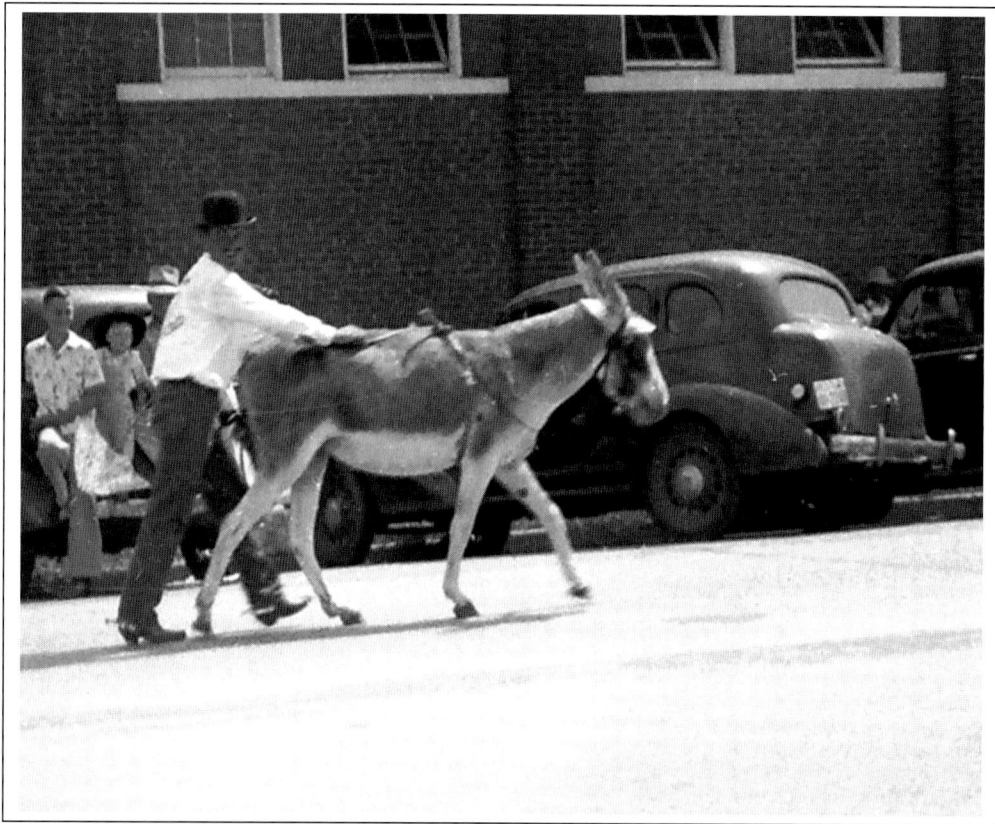

John Lindsey entertains spectators during a Rodeo Parade down Ada's Main Street. Lindsey was one of nation's most famous Rodeo Clowns.

The Clowns —

Rodeo Clown John Lindsey was always a crowd favorite in parades and during rodeo performances.

Clowns were a vital part of rodeos, not only for entertainment but also to provide safety for rodeo performers. Most rodeo clowns adopted circus-like clown makeup and outlandish costumes. Although the clowns provided great entertainment with some of their performances, protecting a downed bull rider was very important. Riders on horses could not because the loose bulls would gore the horses. The rodeo clowns became the unsung heroes who distracted the bulls while thrown riders could escape.

Lindsey was among the favorite clowns and a regular at the Ada Rodeo for many years. He was a veteran clown, who started rodeoing in 1921 and began clowning in 1927 (Klepper 2009).

Lindsey used a miniature Hereford bull, "Iron Ore," with his act; and a trained mule, "Hoover," in parades. Lindsey was inducted into the National Cowboy Hall of Fame in 1986.

*End of the road—
Heavy rains and
resulting floodwaters
"washed out" a
bridge on Big Sandy
Creek, west of Ada.*

The Wintersmith Park Amphitheatre, built into a natural slope on the south edge of Wintersmith Park, consists of natural stone from the park area and other stones quarried from the Fittstown area, southeast of Ada. The Amphitheatre was built by stonemasons of the Civilian Conservation Corps (CCC), working under the supervision of the National Park Service. Many community events, including plays, musicals, public speaking and community sings were held at the site.

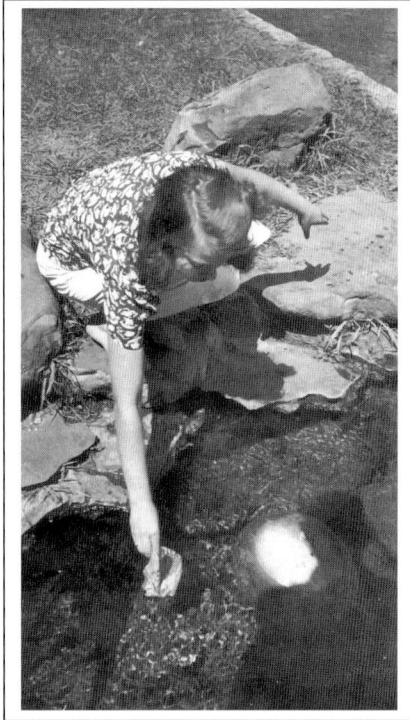

Maxine dipping fresh spring water at the edge of Wintersmith Lake.

Girl cautiously boarding a rental fishing boat.

Draining Wintersmith Lake —

A build up of algae in the water in Wintersmith Lake and sediment at the dam created a need to "drain, clean and refill" the lake in the late 1940s. The unsightly pictures of the drained lake differed significantly from that of the beautifully restored lake. The 15-acre Wintersmith Lake is part of a 150-acres park that was constructed in 1934-1935 by the Civilian Conservation Corps (CCC) under National Park Service supervision.

A restored beautiful Wintersmith Park Lake

Children and parents fill every seat for a Sunday afternoon ride on the miniature train at Wintersmith Park, Ada, Oklahoma.

Begging for Treats —
The City of Ada maintained a small zoo at Wintersmith Park for a few years in the late 1940s. The monkeys were among the most popular animals. The closeness of the monkeys to zoo visitors encouraged monkeys to reach for treats, and the sign cautioned visitors to keep their distance from the cage.

Weatherworn rocks, blackjack and post-oak trees covered a vast rustic area east of Ada. Pieces of petrified wood could be found throughout this area. Delbert "rides down" a small tree.

A small cave in the weathered rocks east of Ada, Oklahoma

Rugged Cross Timbers —

The Northern Cross Timbers is a wide belt of land stretching from south-central Oklahoma into southeastern Kansas, consisting of many trees believed to be 200 to 400 years old. The woodland and savanna portions of the Cross Timbers are mainly post oak and blackjack oak trees growing on coarse, sandy soils. The Cross Timbers earned its name from settlers who found much of the thick forests impassable as Indian Territory and Oklahoma Territory were opened for settlement.

American writer Washington Irving passed through the area in 1832 and wrote of the "vexations of flesh and spirit" that set upon the travelers who he said felt as if they were "struggling through forests of cast iron." Irving's encounter with the West came in 1832 when he accompanied the Commissioner of Indian Affairs on a month-long journey to what is now eastern Oklahoma. His account of that trip, *A Tour on the Prairies* (1835), described wild landscape, rugged inhabitants, and dramatic chases and hunts with an eye for romantic sublimity and a keen appreciation of the frontiersman's "secret of personal freedom."

— *(Irving, Washington, 1886. A Tour of the Prairies. John B. Alden, New York. pp. 78-79)*

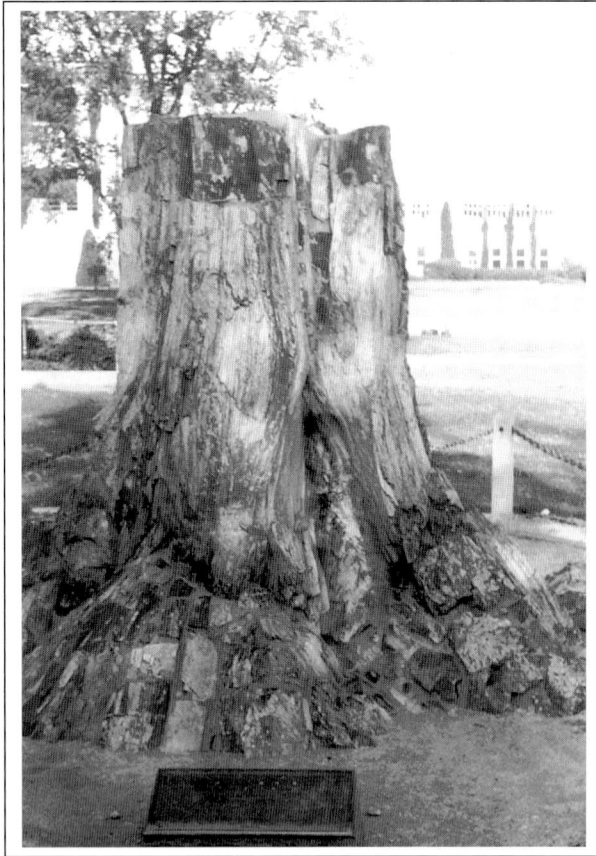

A 350-million-year-old Callixylon tree sits at the entrance to East Central State College campus. The petrified tree was uncovered on farmland near Ada and is reported to be the largest example of the first forest trees in the world.

The Callixylon Tree —

In the years between 1913 and 1936, East Central State College and the Smithsonian Institution in Washington, D.C., vied for the fossil Callixylon tree that had been discovered on farmland near Ada. The tree was reported to be the largest example of a petrified tree.

Dr. David White, head of the U.S. Geological Survey, examined the fossil and decided it should be displayed at the Smithsonian. College supporters raised money for erecting the tree fragments into a tree shape and moving it to the campus. Dr. White died before enough funds had been raised to move the tree to the Smithsonian. As a result, the tree was given to East Central State College and was formally accepted by Dr. Adolph Linscheid, the college president, in March 1936.

Abandoned farm wagon on the Norris Estate, east of Ada, Oklahoma
— 1948

Chapter Two

Family and Neighborhood —

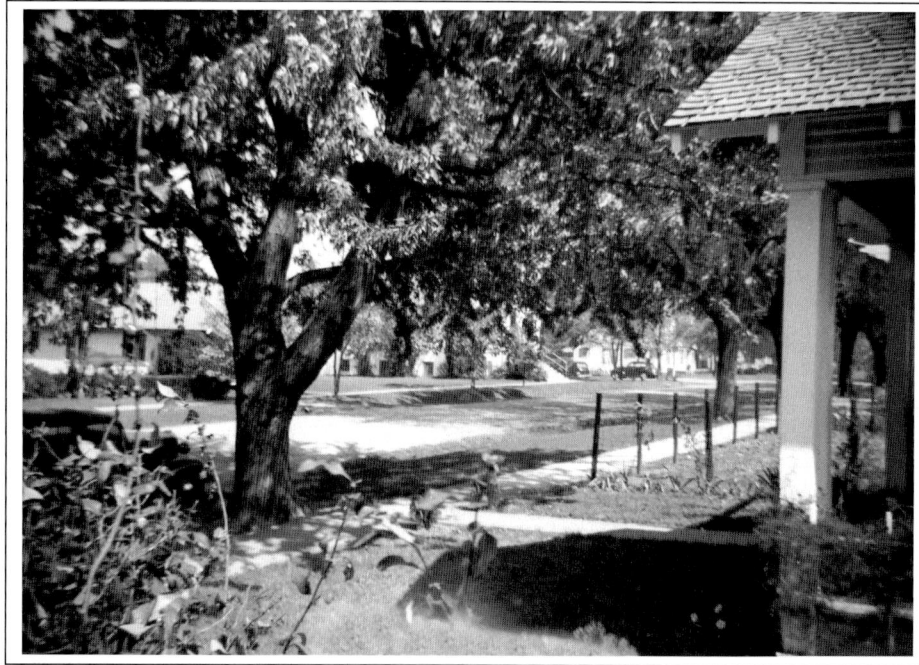

View of tree-shaded neighborhood in the 500 block of West Sixth Street in Ada, Oklahoma, from the Oliver's' front porch, looking east toward Asbury Methodist Church.

Jewell (Dyer-Roberts) Oliver, Clarence's mother, with M. D. L. Roberts, the man who "adopted" an orphaned Jewell at age six months after both her parents died in an influenza epidemic. View from the front yard of the Oliver's' home on West Sixth Street, Ada, Oklahoma. The car in the background is a 1936 Hudson coupe, owned by a lady who for a short period rented a bedroom from the Olivers.

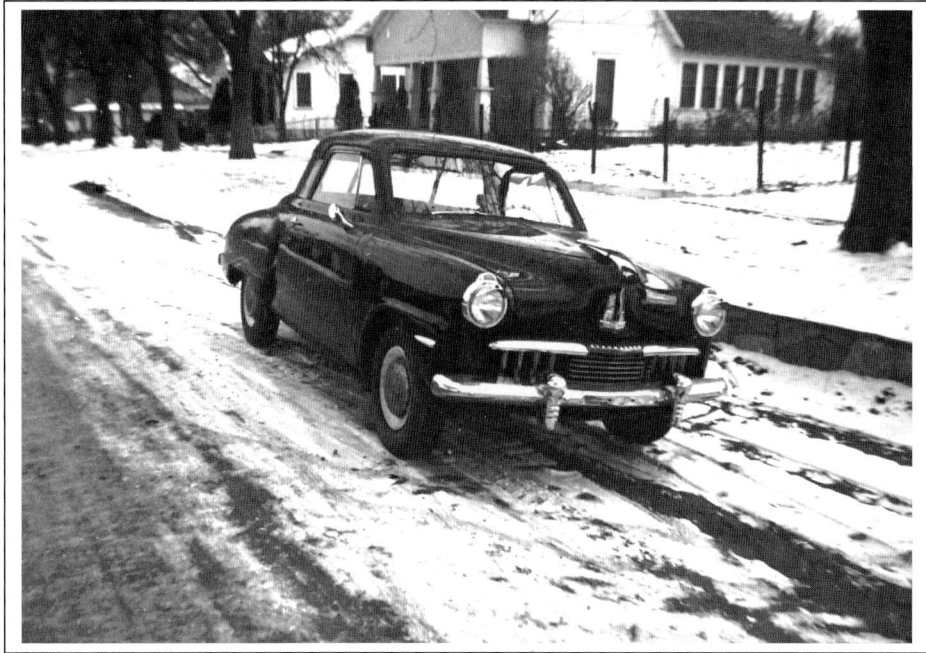

1947 Studebaker Starlight Coupe —
The new family car purchased by Fred and Mabel Jones, next-door neighbors to the Olivers, caught the
attention of all the neighbors because of its innovative new design. The Studebaker was one of the most
impressive of the post-World War II autos.

1947 Studebaker Starlight Coupe —

When neighbor's Fred and Mabel Jones brought home their new 1947 Studebaker Starlight Coupe, high school senior Clarence Oliver, Jr. thought that was the "best looking car" ever designed. The new car was the "talk of the neighborhood." Fred Jones, an auto mechanic, had chosen one of the most impressive and innovative of the post-World War II cars.

The Studebaker Company had prepared well in advance for the anticipated post-war market and launched the slogan *"First by far with a post-war car."* The Starlight coupe was a unique two-door body style and was offered by the company from 1947 to 1952. The car's body style was designated as a five-passenger coupe, distinguishing it from the three-passenger businessman's coupe of other auto companies.

Unlike other pillared two-door sedans with two side windows separated from the rear window by roof supports, Starlight coupe's designer created a rounded (at the rear) roof with a wraparound window system that provided a panoramic effect, similar to a railroad observation car. The curved window was achieved with four fixed panels of glass. Two wide pillars immediately behind the doors and in front of the wraparound back window supported the roof. The body style was originally named, simply, "5-passenger coupe" however, starting with the 1949 model year, it was re-named Starlight Coupe.

The innovative styling influenced later cars, including the flat-back "trunk" instead of a tapered look of the time, and a wrap-around rear window. The new trunk design prompted a running joke that one could not tell if the car was "coming or going."

The Studebaker Company was founded in 1852 in South Bend, Indiana, and the company originally produced wagons for farmers, miners and the military. The first gasoline cars to be manufactured by Studebaker were marketed in August 1912. Over the next 50 years, the company established an enviable reputation for quality and reliability. The South Bend plant ceased production on December 20, 1963, and the last Studebaker car rolled off the Hamilton, Ontario, Canada, plant on March 16, 1966—the end of an era.

Clarence Oliver, Jr.
Senior year, Ada High School
—1947

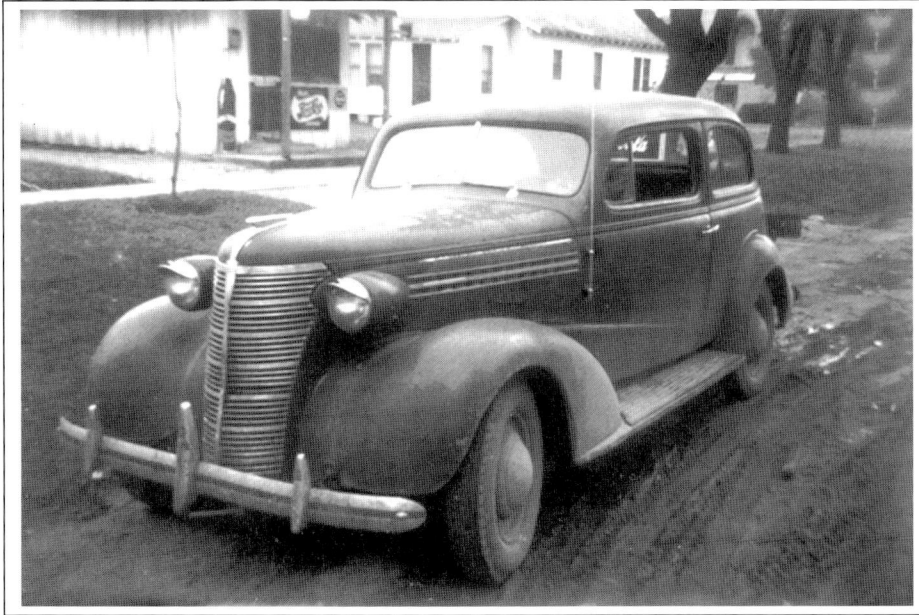

1938 Chevrolet Sedan —
The Oliver's family car, parked on a muddy street in front of the home on West Sixth Street. M.D.L.
Roberts' small neighborhood grocery store is pictured in the background.

M. D. L. Roberts—"Grand-dad"

His friends called him Marcus. His wife usually referred to him as Fayte. Most papers related to his business activities listed him as M. D. L. Roberts. Legally, his name was Marquis de Lafayette Roberts—so named in recognition of a great French nobleman who endeared himself to Americans with his heroic service during the Revolutionary War.

M. D. L. Roberts was Clarence Oliver's "Grandfather." Perhaps he was not that relationship legally since he and his wife, Selena, who died before Clarence was born, did not formally adopt the six-month old orphan girl they took to raise as their own. That girl was Jewell Dyer —Clarence's mother. She was known all her life as the Roberts' daughter. There was never a legal adoption.

Even though he went blind while a mid-30's adult, he managed to work and support his family, eventually opening and operating a small neighborhood grocery store. He played a harmonica, mouth harp, sang, composed poetry—and helped young Clarence to develop the skill of "seeing with the mind's eye."

The Oliver Home on West Sixth Street —
The early 1900s house had few changes until the late 1940s
when the front porch was removed, replaced with a concrete porch
and later a new porch top (canopy) was added and the house was
painted.

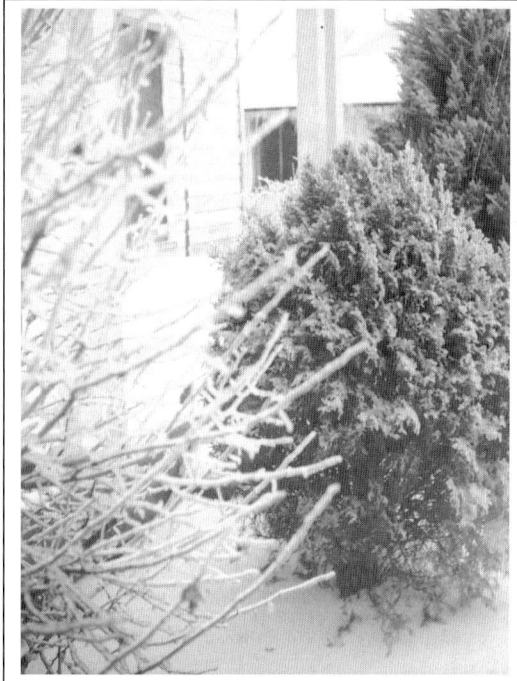

Winter's Fury —
The entire state of Oklahoma was under an
icy blanket for several days in late January
1949. Many cities were without power,
schools were closed, traffic was halted, and
roofs failed under the weight of ice and
snow. Five inches of sleet was recorded,
"The Ada Evening News" reported in the
January 28, 1949 edition. Snow and sleet
drifted on the north side and blocked the
front entrance of the Oliver home.

Little Sister at Play —
Jane Alice Oliver enjoyed "playing Mommy" with a new
doll and some new play furniture, hand-crafted by Dad,
Clarence Oliver, Sr.
— Spring 1948

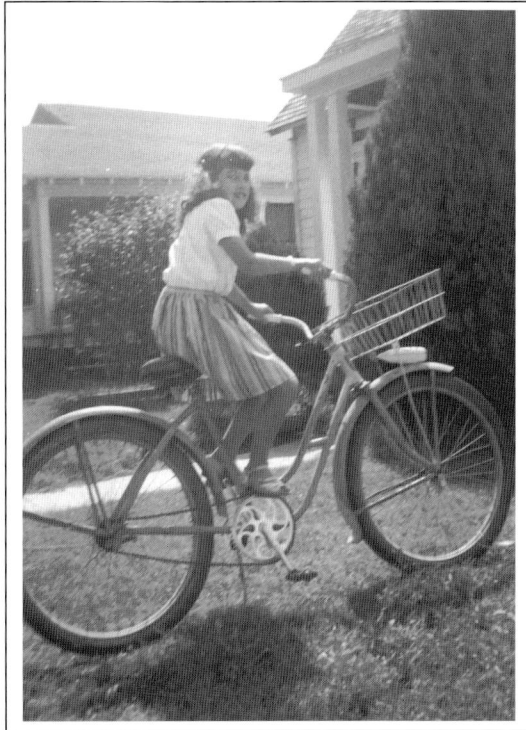

"New" Bike —
Jane Alice Oliver, age nine, became the proud owner of a Schwinn bicycle, equipped with headlight on front fender, basket and side kickstand. Cash-strapped Dad located a used bicycle, bought it for $5.00, then completely overhauled and carefully painted the bicycle. Jane's short stature didn't let her feet reach the pedals while sitting on the bike's seat, so all "rides" were done while pedaling standing up.
— Spring 1948

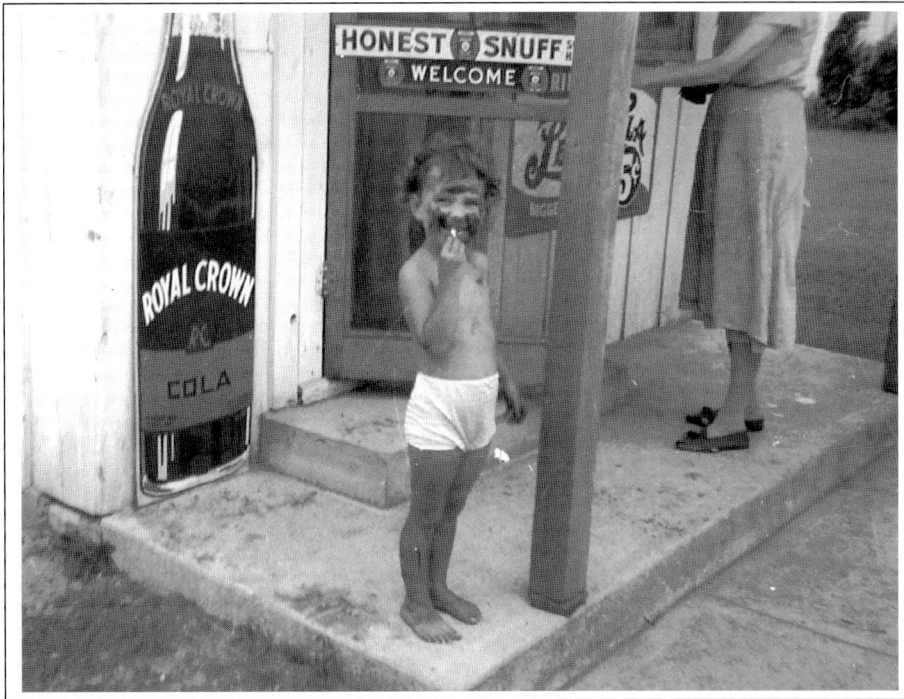

Baby Sister—
Jane Alice Oliver, with Mom's lipstick in hand, in front of Grand-dad Roberts'
neighborhood store.

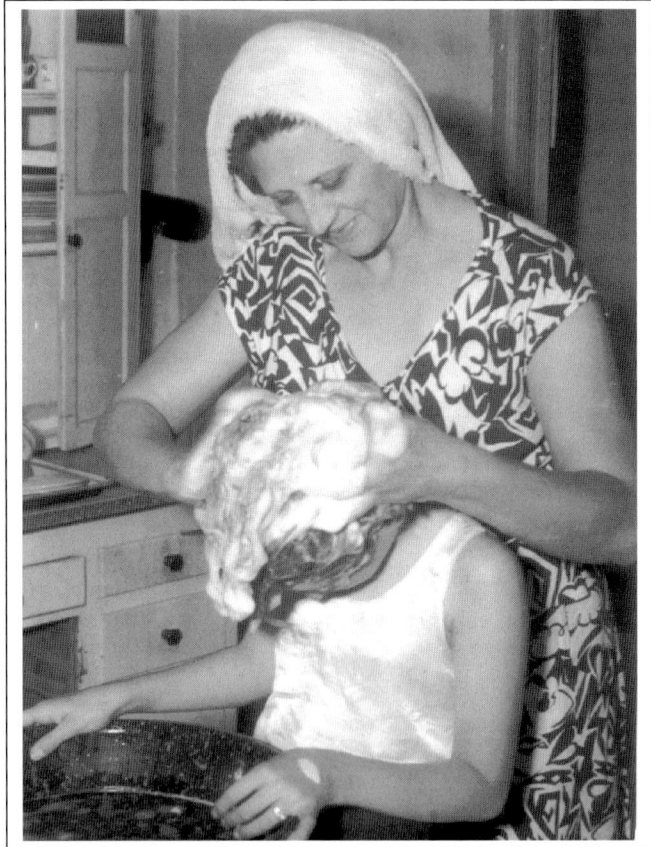

Shampoo time —
Mother and daughter, Jewell Oliver
and Jane Alice, in kitchen at the
Oliver home.

Mom and Dad —
Jewell Americus (Dyer-Roberts) Oliver
and
Clarence G. Oliver, Sr.

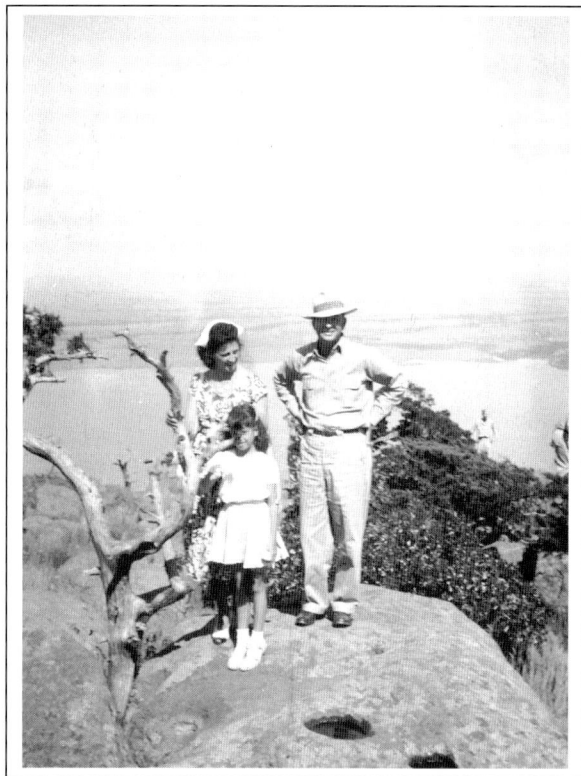

On Top of Mount Scott—
Mom, Dad and Little Sister on top of
Mount Scott in Wichita Mountains of
western Oklahoma.
                              — August 1948

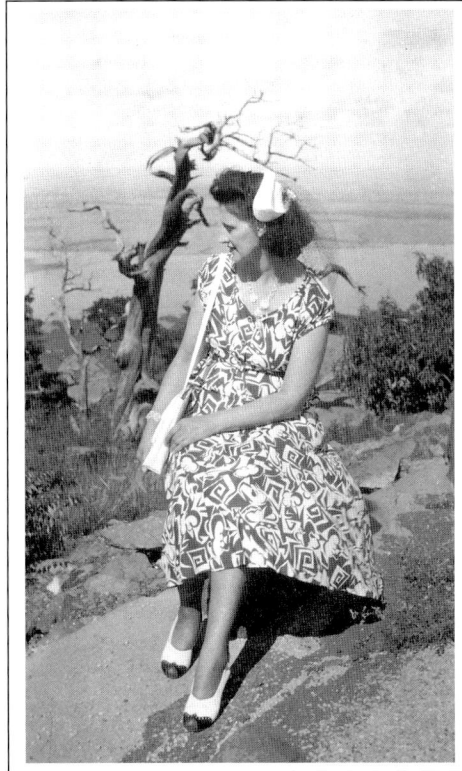

Mom —
Jewell Oliver enjoys view of the Wichita
Mountains and Lake Lawtonka from
top of Mount Scott in western
Oklahoma.

Thanksgiving Day —
Aunt Delia and Uncle Chester Mathis hosted Thanksgiving Day dinner at their country home, north of Ada,
inviting the Olivers. Granddad Roberts, Delia's father and Mom's adopted father, sits in place of honor, with
Mom, Sister Jane Alice and Dad on right.

— November 1949

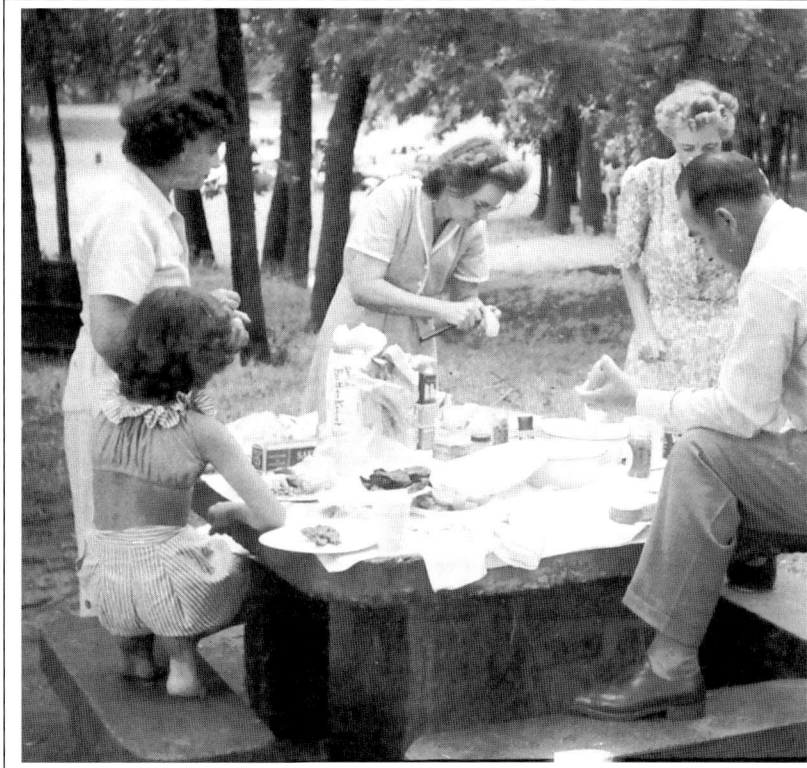

Picnic in Oklahoma City Park —
The Olivers, Jewell, Jane Alice, and Clarence, Sr., enjoy an outing with life-long
friends, sisters Eunice (Neal) Tate and Lexia Neal.

Girlfriends for Life —
Eunice (Neal) Tate and Jewell (Dyer-Roberts) Oliver were close friends during their teen years, and
remained friends for the rest of their lives. A ride on the carousel during a family outing in Oklahoma City
in the Summer 1949 let them recall days of their youth.

On a Carousel Horse —
Jane Alice Oliver sits all alone on Carousel at an Oklahoma City park during a family
outing to the Capital City.

Shirley Family Reunion —
A rare gathering on July 4, 1950, brought together most of the surviving brothers and sisters of the
Shirley family, along with spouses and children. Vinita Shirley, her parents, Sally and Lee Shirley, and
younger brother, Charles, are at left in the photograph. Others are sister Anne Shirley, the Mary Ruth
(Shirley) and Charles Frost family, and Jay and Dorothy Shirley.

Sisters and Cousins —
Vinita Shirley, right, joins
her four cousins from the
Frost family during a Shirley
family reunion on July 4,
1950

Frost sisters: Ruth Ann,
Betty Jean, Constance
Yvonne, and Mary Lois.

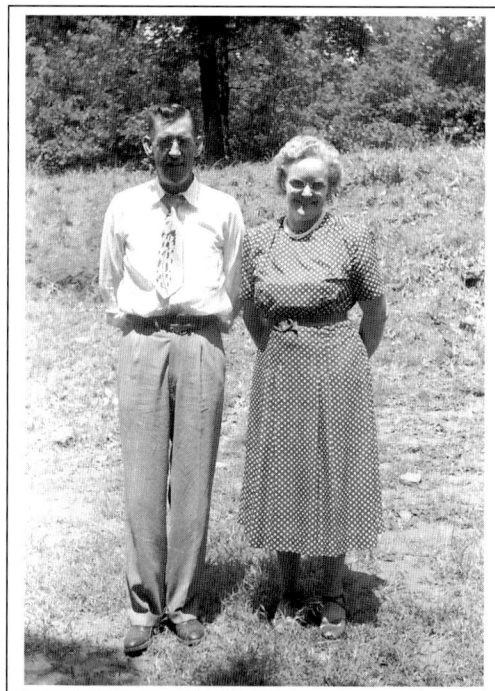

Brothers and Wives —
Jay and Dorothy Shirley, left, and Lee and Sally Shirley pose during a Shirley family reunion.

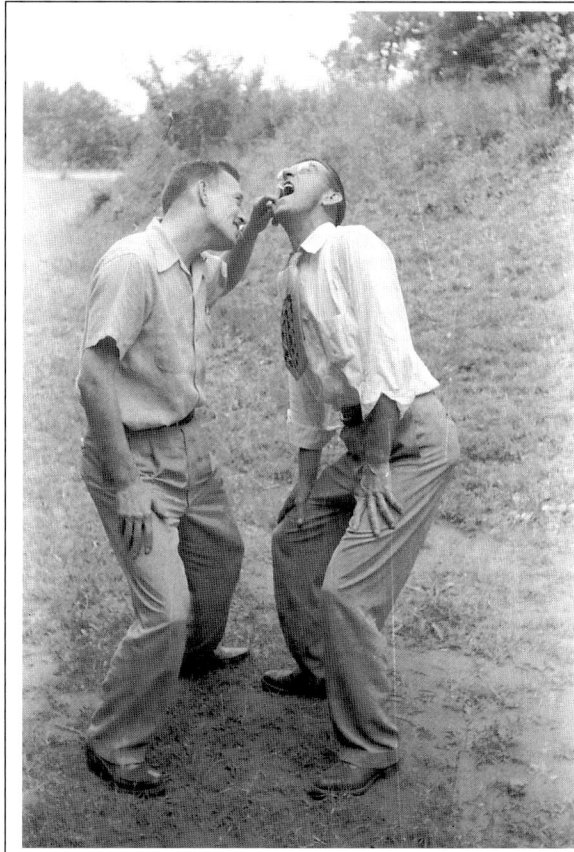

*New Dentist in Town —
Dr. Jay Shirley, left, recently
graduated from dental school, does
an "out-of-office" check up of his
older brother, Lee Shirley, during
a Shirley family reunion on July 4,
1950.*

Chapter Three

Searching for Career —

First Published Newspaper Picture —

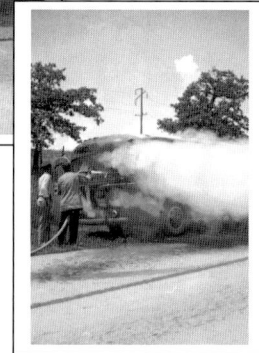

News Photographer —

On July 19, 1948, a Denco Bus Company bus caught fire from an engine problem while enroute to Ada. This incident provided the occasion for Oliver's first published newspaper photograph.

Oliver was working at Stansel Studio when he heard a report that a passenger bus was on fire on a highway north of Ada. He grabbed the small personal camera that was always nearby and drove to the site where he found the burning bus with the driver and passengers standing by the side of the highway. Several pictures were snapped and Oliver rushed back to the studio, quickly developed the film, made prints from wet negatives and took several prints to the Ada Evening News office, just one block north of the studio.

The news editor selected one of the pictures for that afternoon's newspaper. The first published print, and other pictures taken at the scene, are shown.

Other such opportunities, such as an airplane crash that claimed the lives of four members of a prominent Ada banking family, followed.

Front Page News Photo —
Oliver's first published news photograph, complete
with a "byline," made the front page of the Ada
Evening News of July 19,1948.

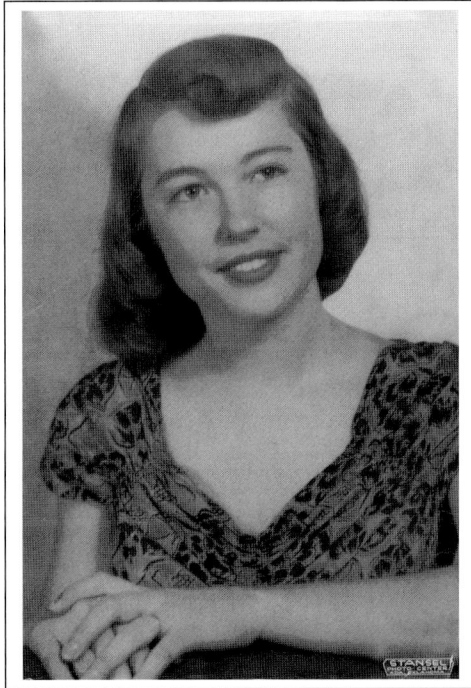

First Solo Professional Portrait —

Working as an apprentice to professional photographer James Stansel permitted Clarence Oliver to learn a great deal about photography as a career. He studied the business at all levels, from roll film developing and contact prints to advanced portrait and commercial photography.

In the spring of 1949, Oliver was given the opportunity for his first solo professional portrait assignment—appointment, lighting, camera selection, posing and taking a variety of photographs, developing film, retouching, final prints and sales.

Maxine Kemp, at friend at church and school, was the subject. She was well pleased with her portrait photos, including this favorite pose that she selected for the newspaper announcement of her engagement.

Engagement Announced —
The engagement of Miss Maxine Rae Kemp to Mr. James Bradley Badgett, with the accompanying portrait photograph, appeared in the Ada Evening News on Sunday, May 9, 1949. They were married on June 7, 1949.

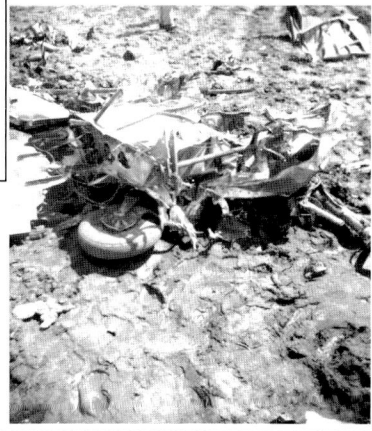

Four members of a prominent Ada banking family died when their private airplane exploded and crashed on Sunday, April 13, 1947. Wreckage of the four-place Navion plane is pictured, stewn across plowed farm land south of Ada.

The Ada Evening News
— April 14, 1947

Documenting a Tragedy —

Tragedy struck a prominent Ada banking and business family on Sunday afternoon, April 13, 1947, when their airplane exploded and crashed on a farm near the Pecan Grove School, south of Ada. The dead in the crash were Frank Norris, 38, president of the First National Bank of Ada; his wife, Wilma; a brother, Tom Norris, Paris, Texas, and the latter's wife, Virginia.

The owner and pilot of the plane was Tom Norris, a World War II air forces veteran. The four were returning to Ada from a weekend visit in Hot Springs, Arkansas. The men were sons of the late P.A. Norris, Ada banker who had extensive holdings in banks, cottonseed oil companies and other businesses in Oklahoma and North Texas. The senior Mr. Norris died in 1942.

The airplane disaster was the worst in Pontotoc County's history of aviation. Hundreds of people drove to the crash scene to see the remnants of the plane that was scattered along three-quarters of a mile of farmland.

The editor of The Ada Evening News did not choose Oliver's free-lance news photos of the crash scene for publication.

Oak Avenue Baptist Church Vacation Bible School
— Summer 1950

Going it Alone —

Oliver struck out on his own as a free-lance photographer during the summer of 1950, with hopes of earning money to return for his senior year at Oklahoma A and M College in Stillwater, Oklahoma. He and his father turned a corner of his bedroom into a small darkroom. Oliver purchased a used Speed Graphic camera, tripod, enlarger, lights, darkroom supplies and with a homemade contact printer, he was "in business."

These photographs of the Vacation Bible School students and teachers at Oak Avenue Baptist Church and Asbury Methodist Church, portraits of Anne Carroll, daughter of Rev. and Mrs. Jack Carroll, and photographs of the Fred Jones family are examples of his summer free-lance work.

Asbury Methodist Church Vacation Bible School
— Summer 1950

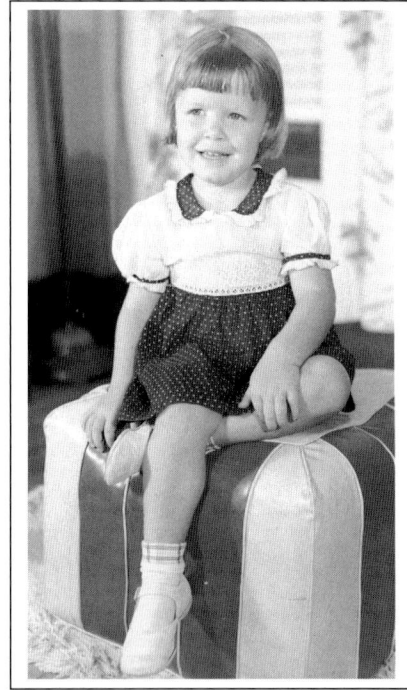

Anne Carroll, daughter of Rev. and Mrs. Jack Carroll.

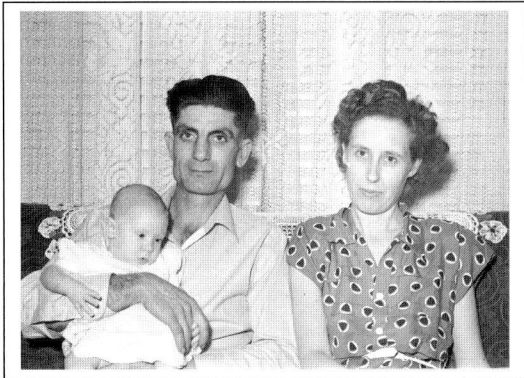

Fred and Mabel Jones with their young son, Fred Wayne.

Chapter Four

The "Gang" —

Through the Smoke —
One of many nighttime picnics enjoyed by "the Gang," sitting around a log fire, talking and eating.

"The Gang" —

The term, "Gang," had a very innocent meaning during the 1940s—most certainly in Ada, Oklahoma.

"The Gang" was a close-knit group of young people from school and church, but mostly from Oak Avenue Baptist Church. This was a group of about a dozen close friends, all whom lovingly described themselves as, "The Gang."

This was a group with a very special relationship. They often piled into one car, usually the Oliver's 1938 Chevrolet sedan, for evening drives, picnics, parties, trips to the Kit-Kat drive-in for hamburgers and Cokes, and scores of other activities that are so important to young people.

Sometimes five or six were together and sometimes eight or nine were together—in one or two cars, depending on what was available. In the beginning, they were just friends. Later, some dating couples emerged. But, for three or four years, this was just a group of special friends, some of whom maintained life-long connections.

Friends —

Dorothy Mills,
Betty See,
Giles Mitchell,
Vinita Shirley and
Ed Haley

Bundled up and ready to leave the Oliver home for a winter evening —
Ed Haley, Mary Nell Turley, John Turley, Betty Mitchell, Clarence Oliver, Betty See,
Delbert Marshall and Giles Mitchell

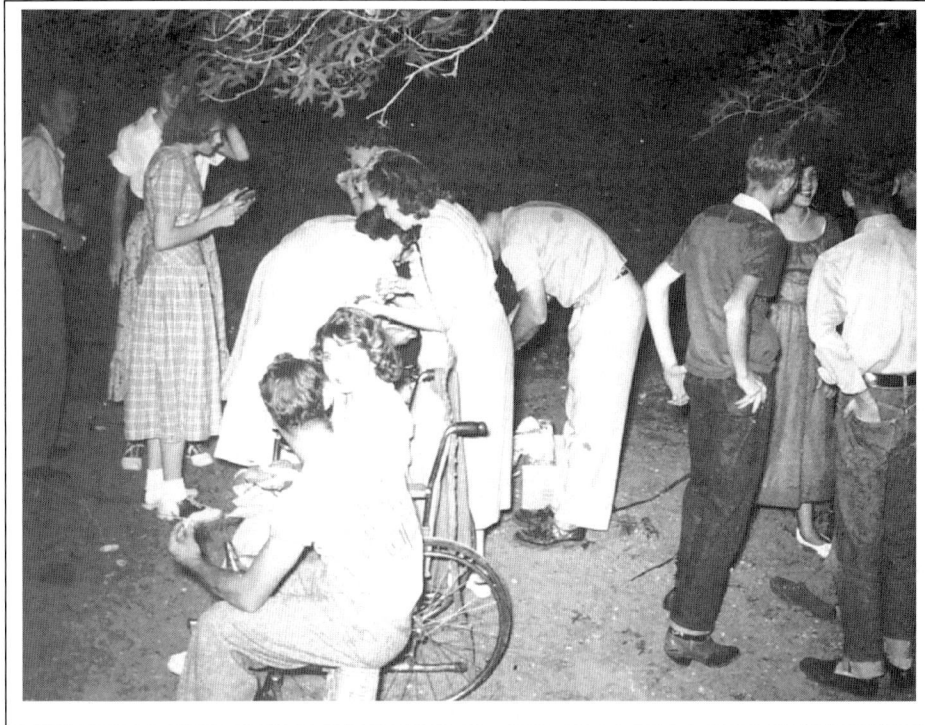

Nighttime Picnic at Wintersmith Park —

Vinita and Mary Nell —
Wading in Pennington Creek in the
Devil's Den park area.

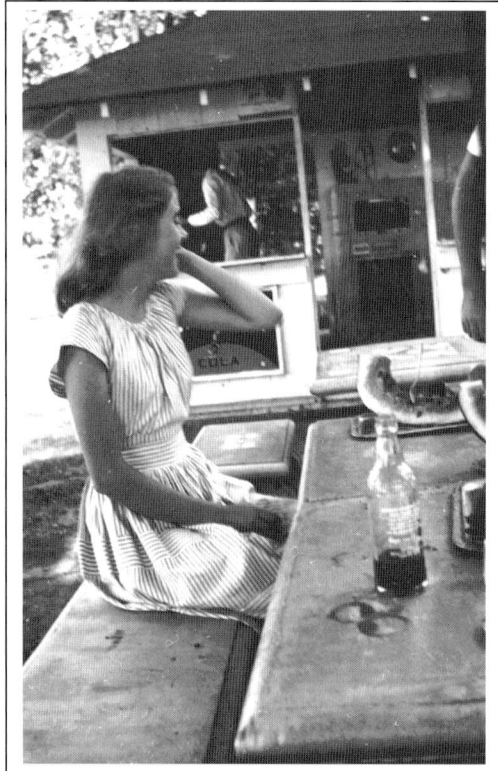

Vinita —
At the Watermelon Stand on
North Broadway

The Jukebox —

Inside the building is a Wurlitzer—the iconic jukebox of the Big Band era. The large 78-rpm records, with the most popular music of the day, provided great background music, at a price of 10-cents per song or three songs for a quarter.

The first jukeboxes used 78-rpm records exclusively until 1950 when the all 45-rpm jukebox was released. The 45-rpm jukebox soon became the standard for years to come until the advent of digital music and the compact disc.

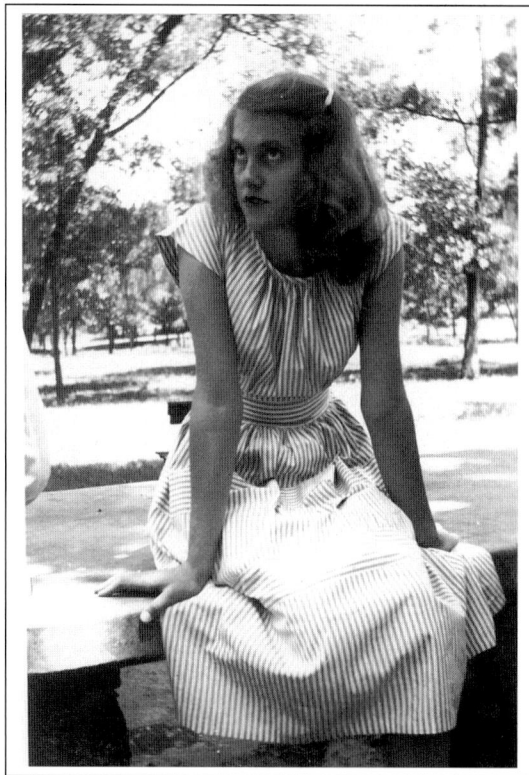

Vinita —
Sitting on table in
Wintersmith Park

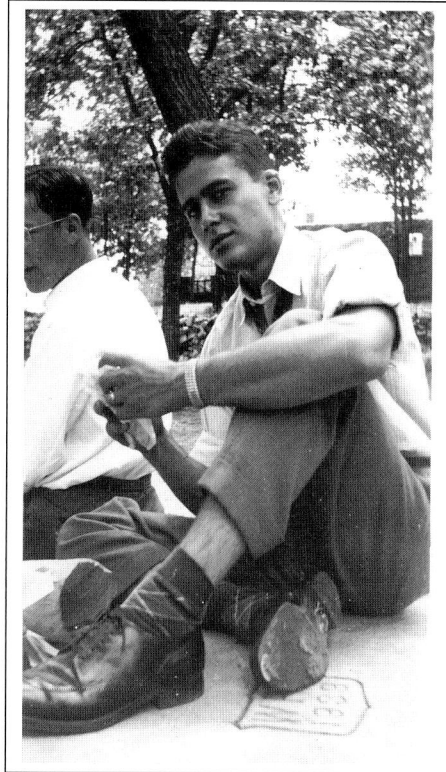

Giles —
At the Watermelon Stand . . .
and in a contemplative mood sitting on a WPA made park table at Wintersmith Park.

Works Projects Administration (WPA) —

On the park table at Wintersmith Park where Giles Mitchell sits as if "contemplating his future" is displayed a shield emblem with "WPA 1938" imprinted in the concrete. The park tables, benches, buildings and many other facilities at the popular Wintersmith Park were the work of men who were employed in the Works Projects Administration (WPA) program.

The Works Progress Administration (renamed in 1939 as the Work Projects Administration—WPA) was the largest New Deal agency, employing millions of people and affecting almost every locality in the United States, especially rural and western mountain populations. It was created by Franklin Delano Roosevelt's presidential order, and funded by Congress with the passage of the Emergency Relief Appropriation Act of 1935 on April 8, 1935.

Between 1935 and 1943, the WPA provided almost eight million jobs. The program built many public buildings, projects and roads and operated large arts, drama, media and literary projects. Almost every community in America has a park, bridge or school constructed by the agency.

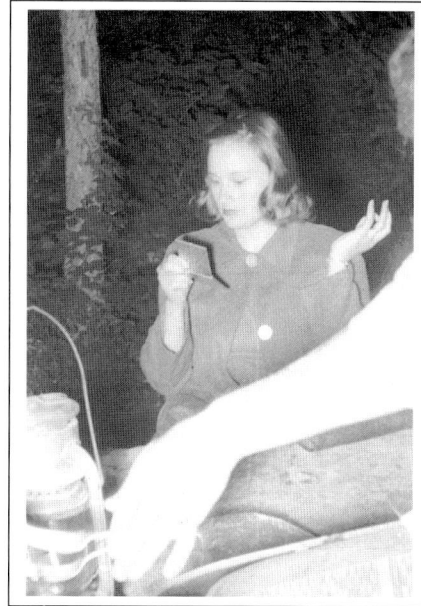

*Betty Mitchell . . . an afternoon in Wintersmith Park
. . . and checking makeup at night by the light of a
kerosene lantern.*

Betty See —
The Rock Gardens at East Central College

Betty and Vinita —
In Wintersmith Park

The Gang —
A Sunday afternoon at Big Sandy Creek
Bridge.

— May 1948

Car parked on the Pennington Creek Bridge

Boys will be boys!

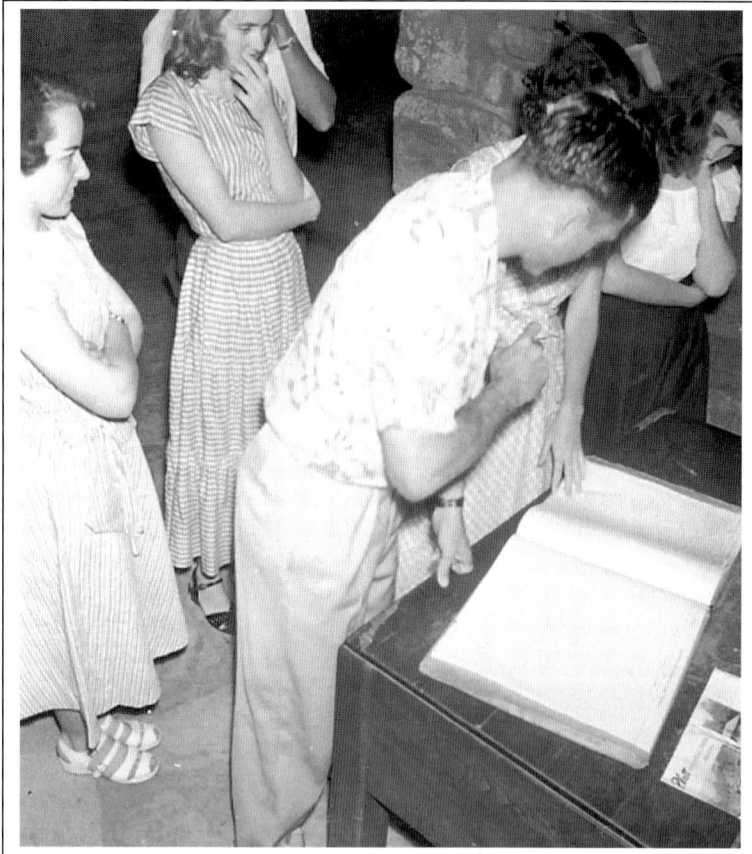

*Checking the Visitors'
Register at Platt
National Park, Sulphur,
Oklahoma.*

Christmas Gift Exchange —
The Gang gathered in the Oliver's home for a gift exchange during a snowy night in 1948.
John and Delbert display gifts. Delbert sports knee high rubber boots used as he walked a
mile through the snow from his home to the party.

"Operator . . . Information Please" —

The standard no-dial black "Bakelite" telephone sits high on a wall shelf in the Oliver's home, with heavy black wires connecting to the large box and bell system.

The Oliver's telephone number was 3144-W, indicating a "party line." A few of the families had three-digit number private lines. Calls were made simply by picking up the handset and giving the operator the number desired.

Operators also were the persons who were asked for "information" on many things besides telephone numbers. They frequently responded to such questions as, "What time is the game tonight?" or "Was the Smith's new baby a boy or girl?"

Life was a bit simpler in those days.

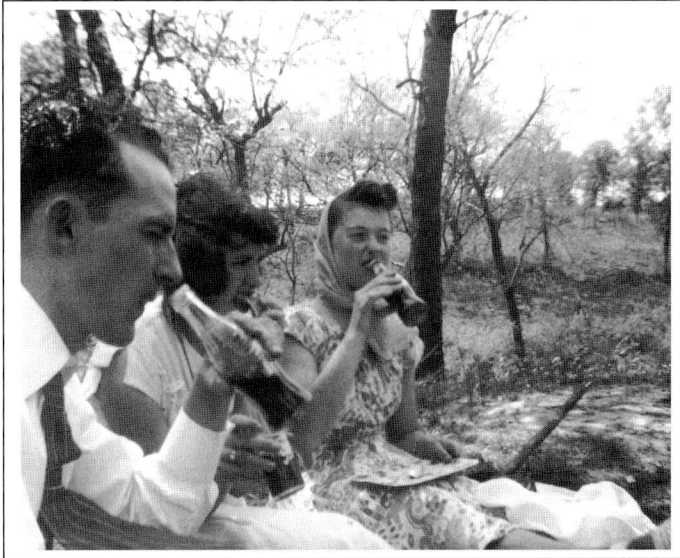

Coke,
Dr. Pepper,
Coke —

Coke was the favored soft drink for the majority of the young people, with Dr. Pepper a close second. The 6-1/2 ounce glass bottle Coke sold for five cents until about 1949 when prices varied from six to 10 cents.

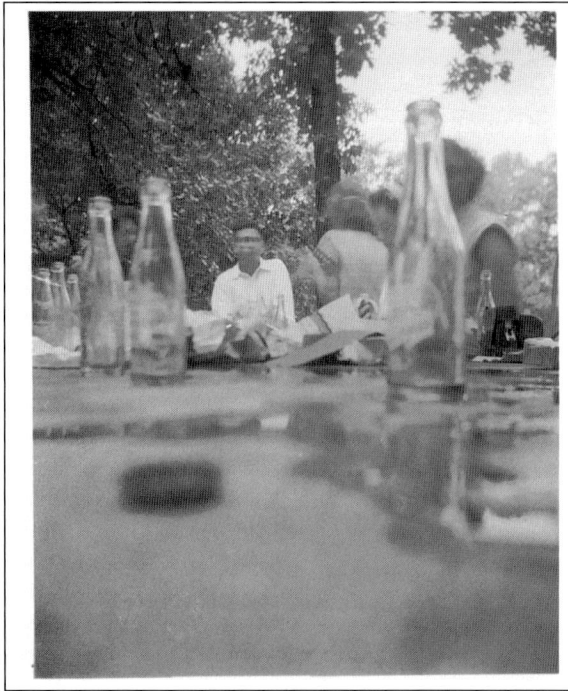

*Empty Soft Drink Bottles —
"Coke" and "Dr. Pepper" were favorite
soft drinks of most young people and cost
five-cents for a six and one-half ounce
bottle. None of the companies offered a diet
variety, an option that would not become
available until the mid-1950's. The empty
bottles were returned to stores for a small
refund and bottles were washed and reused
by bottling companies, often being used 10
to 15 times—or more—before either loss or
breakage retired them from circulation.*

Serene scene on Big Sandy Creek —

The Giant Rocks —
The natural park area
known as Devil's Den
was on private land, but
open to the public during
the 1940s and 1950s.
The vast area was covered
with curiously shaped
rock formations.

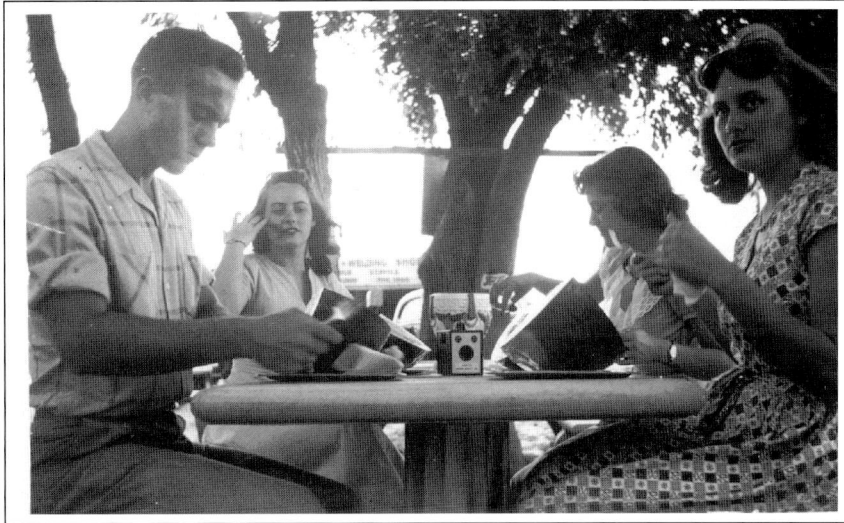

Relaxing in the shade at the Watermelon Stand —
Ed Haley, Mary Nell Turley, Betty See and Betty Mitchell relaxing in the shade.

108

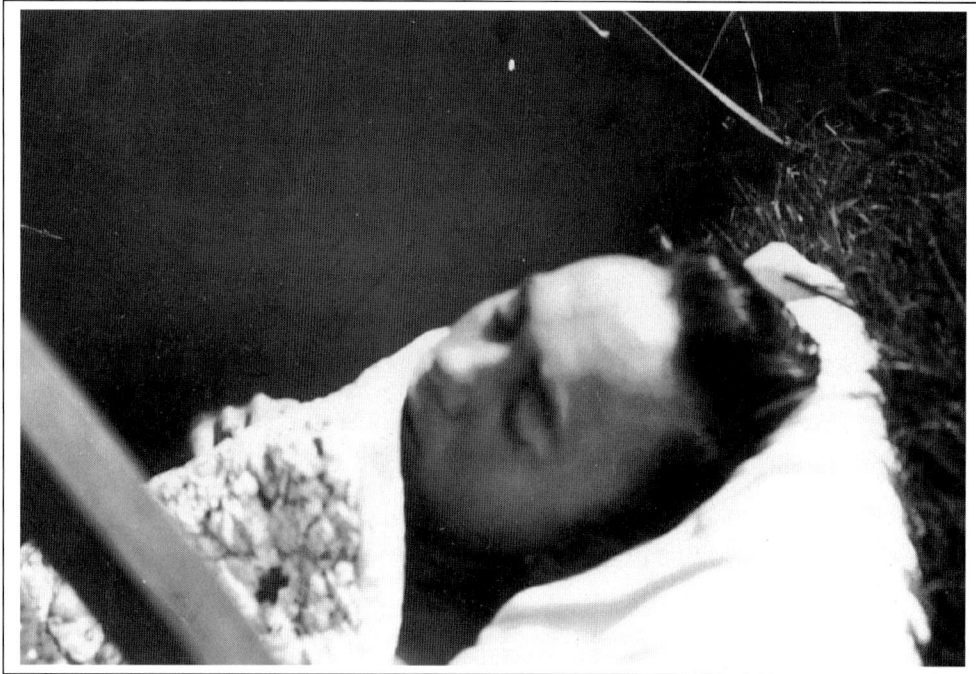

Summertime in Pup Tent —
Ed Haley still snoozes in early morning after spending another night sleeping in a tent in the back
yard of the Haley's home—a common sight during warm summer nights in Oklahoma.

Ben Franklin reincarnated . . .on the streets of Oklahoma City, Oklahoma — 1949.
During a week end trip to "see the sights" in Oklahoma City, Ed reenacts the oft-told tale of
Ben Franklin's arrival in Philadelphia and the story of his wandering around the city with a
loaf of bread under each arm, looking at the buildings and searching for employment.

Giles —

Taking a nap in the shade at Venetian
swimming pool and park, Sulphur,
Oklahoma

Duck Walk —

Two ducks walk at the edge of the swimming pool at Venetian swimming pool and park, Sulphur, Oklahoma.

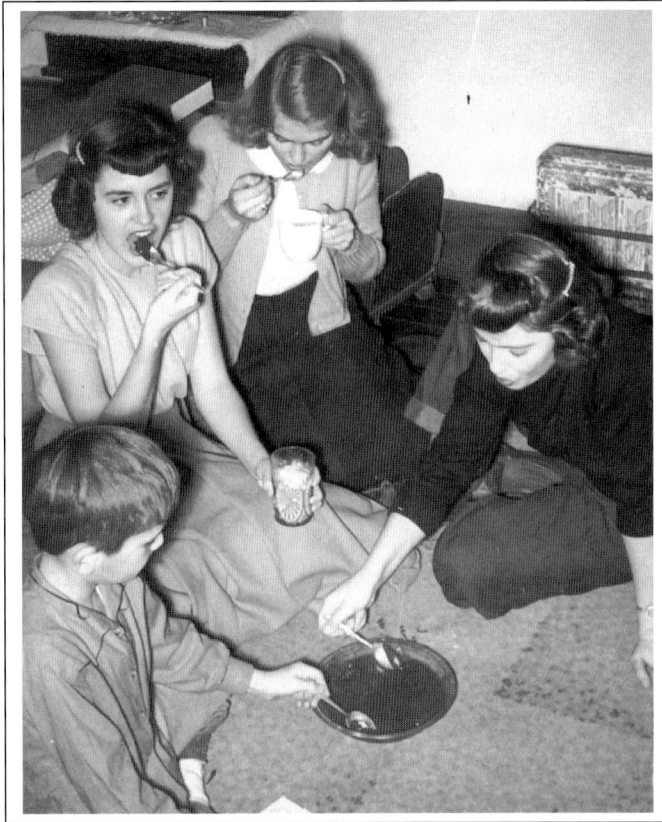

Candy-making Party —

Making chocolate fudge at the See's home.

The fudge didn't get hard this night. Jimmy, Betty, Vinita and Maxine resort to spoons to eat the candy, while enjoying hot chocolate with marshmallows "on the side."

Most homes were heated with open face stoves, similar to the one in the background of this picture. In many homes, often only the "living" room was heated.

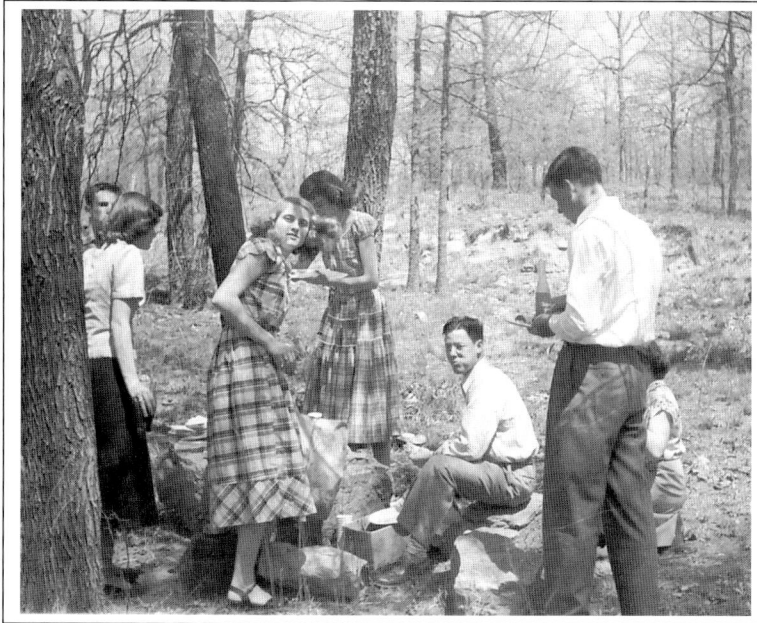

Chow Time in the Woods—
Other people took all the picnic tables at Wintersmith Park so food was "spread on the ground" and no
one minded. Two halves of a pup tent protected the tablecloth from the dirt. Vinita Shirley, Malcolm
Floyd, Wanda Graves, Mary Nell Turley and Bob Bartlett prepare to enjoy an informal lunch.

Summer Scene at Pennington Creek —

High among the rocks in
Devil's Den Park —

Vinita and Mary Nell

Barefoot in the Park —
Vinita enjoying the waters of Pennington Creek.

Vinita and Maxine —
Close friends making plans for Maxine and
J.B.'s approaching summer wedding

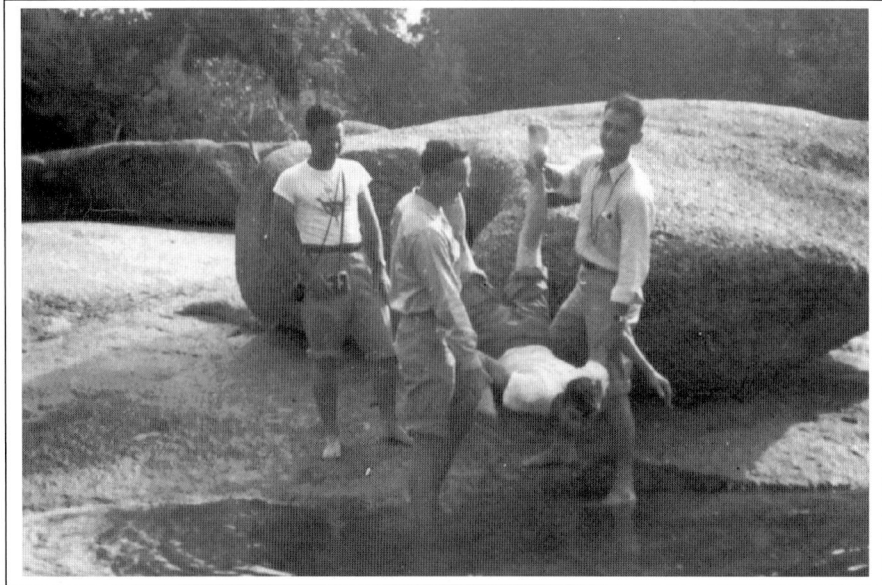

A Playful Moment —
The guys at play in Devil's Den Park

Another of the Gang's "crazy" parties—
Giles Mitchell, Delbert Marshall and Ed Haley sit in front, with Betty Mitchell, Mary Nell
Turley, Betty See and John Turley in back. The Oliver's large Philco AM radio is against the
wall on right side of the photo.

Sunday afternoon time was too good to waste by going home to change into more casual clothing. Shoes off, dress pants "rolled up," and ties removed — and the "guys" were ready to wade, look for minnows, or just enjoy walking barefoot in Pennington Creek at Devil's Den Park.

Early fall afternoon at
Pennington Creek —

Vinita and Mary Nell

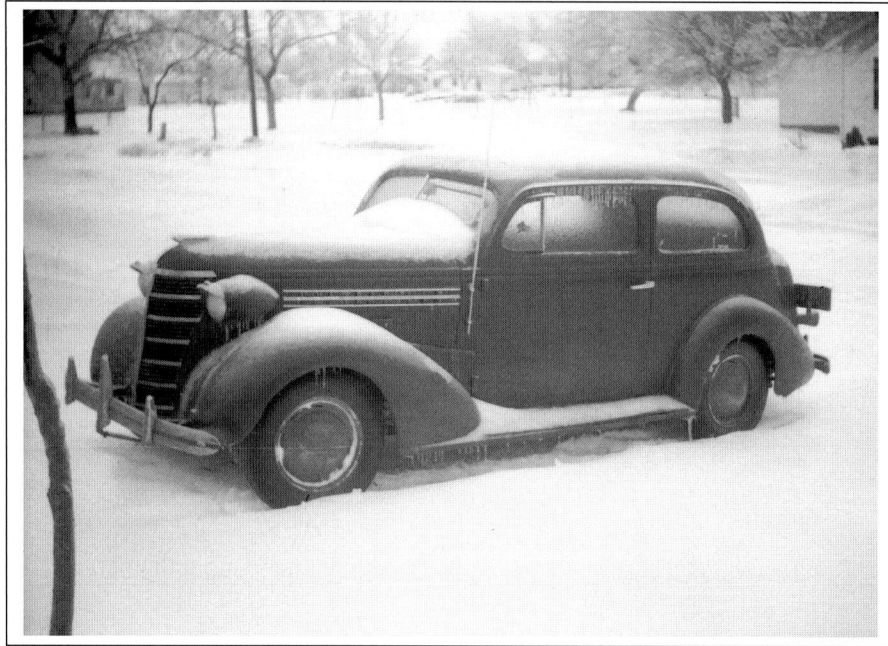

Snowed In —
The infamous "1938 Chevy" frequently used to transport "the Gang" to all kinds
of events and in all kinds of weather. A heavy sleet and snowstorm stopped all traffic
in Ada and around most of the state in late January 1949.

Inside the Oliver family's 1938 Chevrolet Sedan —
The only standard amenity in the car was an AM radio, with overhead speaker. The car didn't have a heater, but an electric heater, operated off the battery-generator system, later was installed under the dash on the passenger side of the car. A dash-mounted fan provided inside air circulation during summer months.

Author's Reflections on "the '38 Chevy" —

During my junior year in high school, my parents, still trying to recover from the loss of many of their worldly possessions during the "Great Depression," purchased a used car—a 1938 two-door Chevrolet sedan that became known in my circle of friends as "the '38 Chevy."

Now, I could "borrow the car" from my parents for a brief period of time to be with friends and to "drag Main."

The '38 Chevy had a stick shift on the floor, with three speeds and a reverse gear. The car had the unique "knee action" front suspension system, a design that eventually proved a bit faulty because it let the wheels lean inward, resulting in excessive wear on the front tires. There was a radio, but the car did not have a heater system. Later, a small electric heater, connected to the car's battery and electrical system, was acquired and installed on the passenger side of the car. That "electric" heater proved ineffective in providing much real warmth in the car, though, and wintertime driving called for the driver and passengers to dress for cold weather both outside and inside the car.

There are a million memories—all good—that are associated with that '38 Chevy. That dependable old green car not only provided transportation for our family, but also provided "wheels" for me during my senior year in high school—and days beyond. Vinita and our friends, "the Gang," piled into that car for evening drives, picnics, parties, trips to the Kit-Kat drive-in for hamburgers and Cokes, and scores of other activities which are so important to young people. It was not unusual for eight of us to be packed into the car.

Three years would pass before Vinita and I would reach the point of an engagement and discussion of marriage. Vinita and I often sat and talked in the '38 Chevy, parked in the driveway in front of the Shirley's home on West Fourth Street, after returning from our frequent dates. Such was the case on a New Year's Eve winter night in 1949 when Vinita said, "Yes," in response to my question, "Will you marry me?"

— The Author

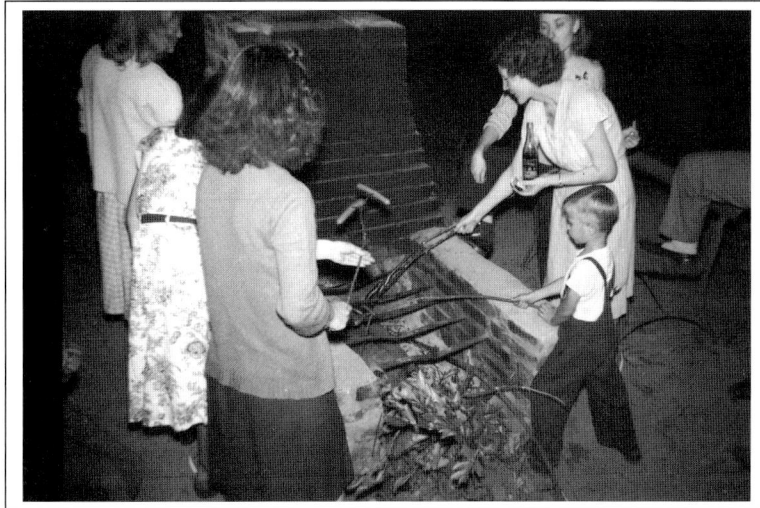

Nighttime "wiener roast" at Wintersmith Park, Ada, Oklahoma.

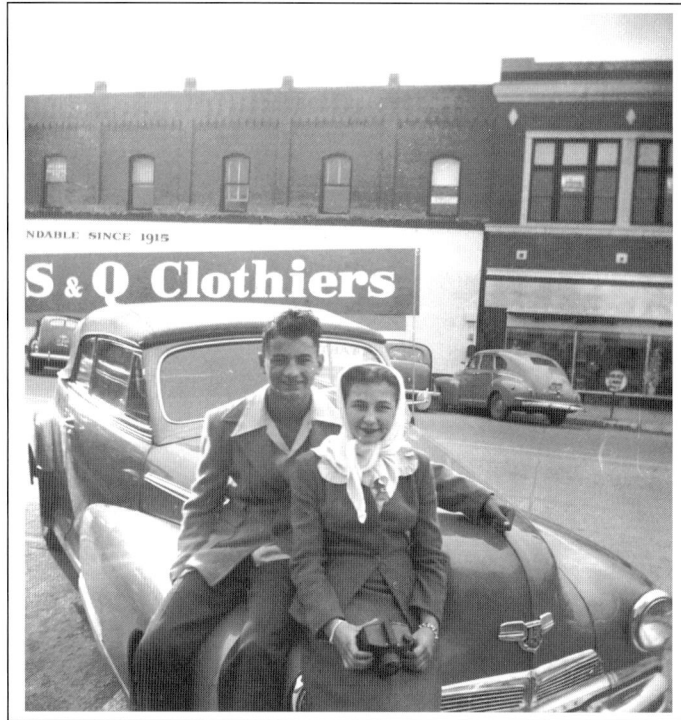

S&Q Clothiers was the premier clothing store for menswear.

Dorothy (Dot) Mills and Clarence Oliver

Reflections on a good day —
Friends in "the Gang" gather in the shadows at the edge of Wintersmith Lake after an afternoon picnic.

Chapter Five

The Church —

Sunday Morning After Church —
Oak Avenue Baptist Church, Ada, Oklahoma, Summer 1946

Sunday Morning After Church —

Looking at a photograph from long ago and speculating about people who are pictured can be an interesting activity.

Such is the case with the photograph of members of the congregation of Oak Avenue Baptist Church as they exit the upstairs church sanctuary after Sunday morning services during which they heard a sermon by the Reverend Chester Mason.

Children run and play. One young mother chases after a small daughter who hasn't been walking too long and is running rapidly near the curb of the street. Young people start to gather in the shade of a tree, probably planning afternoon activities. Women in summer dresses and summer hats gather in twos and threes to visit, some holding babies and others keeping a watchful eye on children.

At the left, two men, one wearing a summer suit, meet in serious discussion—probably about some church business matter. In the center of the photograph, the man in a suit and hat, standing in front of the downstairs entrance to the classrooms and office areas, is in serious thought, perhaps contemplating whether he should "light up a cigarette" that he may have been craving for the past hour.

The year was 1946. A new stage show, "Call Me Mister," opened at National Theater New York City and would run for 734 performances. On April 18, Jackie Robinson debuts as second baseman for the Montreal Royals. The very first bikini bathing suit was displayed in Paris on June 3. The controversial book by Dr. Ben Spock, *Common Sense Book of Baby and Child Care,* was published.

On December 31, President Truman officially proclaims the end of World War II. Life was good. It was "A Time of Peace."

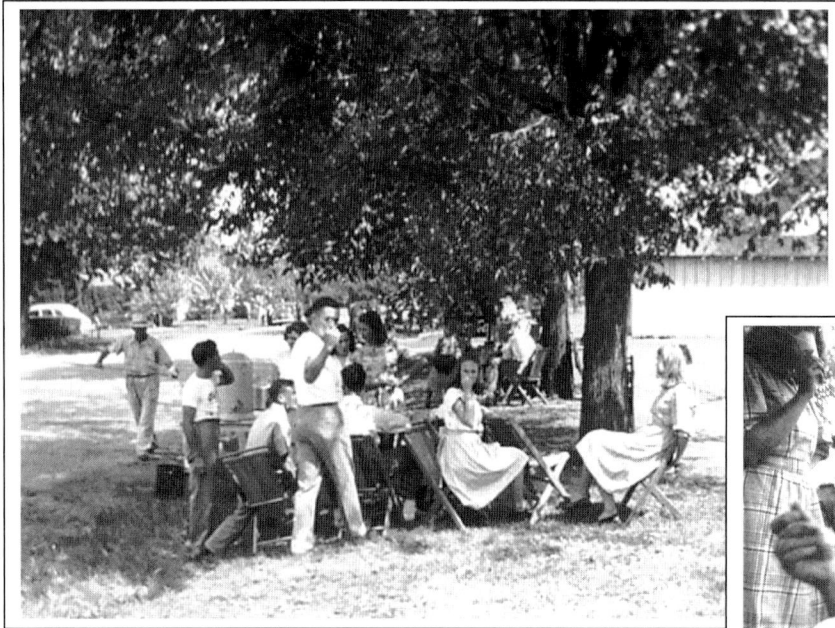

*After church "dinner on the grounds" in the shade
of trees near the pastor's home.*

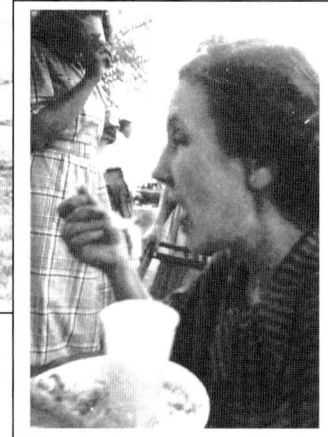

"Dinner on the Grounds" —

Young people, adults and children from Oak Avenue Baptist Church spend time together eating and visiting during a summer "Dinner on the Grounds" for church members and guests following Sunday morning services. The frequent summer social events were held beneath shade trees on the lawn of the church parsonage, located across the street from the church.

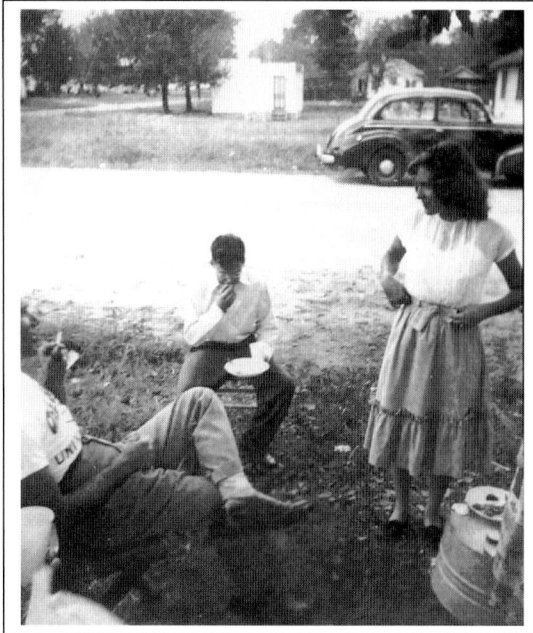

The "Church" provided a common bond for a group of young people who attended Oak Avenue Baptist Church. Just "being together" was a special time for them.

Drama Rehearsal —
Young people of the Baptist Young Peoples Union (BYPU) study group at Oak Avenue
Baptist Church during preparation for a short drama.

Baccalaureate Sunday —
Friends and new high school graduates gather on Sunday afternoon following the 1948 Ada
High School Baccalaureate Service.

Christmas Pageant —
The annual Christmas Pageant involved a large cast—the majority of which were from the young people's Sunday School department. The music, narration, and cast members related the story of the "birth of the Christ child," following closely the story as recorded in the Holy Bible in Luke 2. Pictured is the cast of the 1948 production.

Angel's Wings —
Costumes, makeup, Angel's wings and beards are given last-minute adjustments by Vinita Shirley and Clarence Oliver before they and other cast members enter the auditorium and for the a Christmas pageant program at Oak Avenue Baptist Church, Ada, Oklahoma.

Church Youth Banquet —
Oak Avenue Baptist Church young people's
Sunday School department members, their
guests, youth leaders, Pastor Charles Mason
and his wife, and guest speakers gathered for
banquet events during the year.
— 1948 and 1949

Vacation Bible School Faculty
Oak Avenue Baptist Church.
—1949

Not Exactly a Resort Lodge —
Cabin at Falls Creek Baptist Assembly Grounds near Davis, Oklahoma, where Oak Avenue Baptist
Church youth attendees and sponsors spent two weeks during the Summer 1947.

Youth and sponsors from Oak Avenue Baptist Church at Falls Creek Baptist Assembly near Davis, Oklahoma.

— Summer 1949

Church Secretary—
Vinita Shirley served as the pastor's secretary, general church secretary, "Girl Friday" and "printer." She cranked out programs for Sunday services and a church newsletter using a mimeograph machine at Oak Avenue Baptist Church in Ada. An apron and rubber gloves provided protection from the ink, especially during removal of the used stencils, cleaning the ink drum and work area.

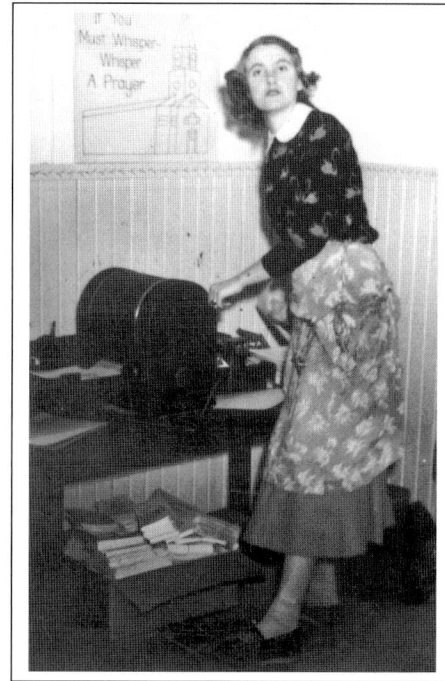

The Mimeograph —

The mimeograph machine, or stencil duplicator, was a low-cost printing press that worked by forcing ink through a stencil onto paper. Along with spirit duplicators and hectographs, mimeographs were for many decades used to print short-run office work, classroom materials and church bulletins. These technologies began to be supplanted by photocopying and offset printing by the late 1960s.

Thomas Edison is credited with inventing the machine and procedure. He obtained a patent for the "Autographic Printing" machine and process in 1876.

Chapter Six

*High School
and College Days —*

Ada Senior High School
— 1947

Science Hall and Main Entrance to East Central College Campus, Ada, Oklahoma.

— 1945

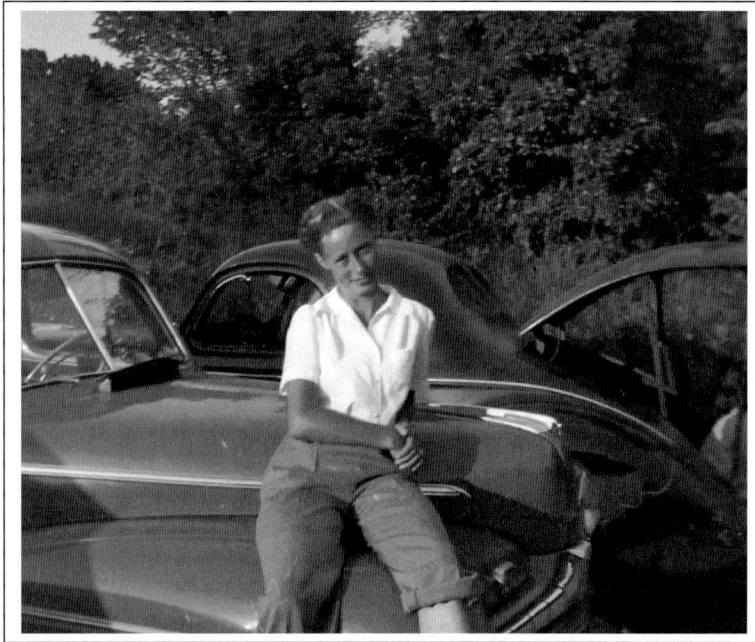

Billie Jean "Slats" Fathree at the Junior-Senior Classes Picnic, 1947

In the background is the Fathree's family car, a 1941-1942 Willys Americar. Coupe

High School Picnic —

Glen Wood, Louella Robinson, Rita Carol Whitsett, Billie Jean Fathree and Clarence Oliver sit on the Fathree's family car, a 1941-42 Willys coupe, at Ada High School Junior-Senior picnic outing.
— May 1947

The Willys Americar —

The 1941-1942 Willys Americar was an ordinary but well-built compact passenger car produced under the presidency of Joseph W. Frazer (later of Kaiser-Frazer) and engineered by Barney Roos. The L-head four-cylinder engine and ladder chassis were conventional, while the sharp-nosed body styling owed a little to previous Hudsons and Nashes.

Prices as low as $634 made the lightweight Americar very competitive. Three variations of the Willys—Speedway, DeLuxe and Plainsman—were offered, each with a coupe and sedan, plus a DeLuxe four-door woody wagon. Production had hardly begun, though, when the company regrouped to build the immortal "Jeep," the important all-purpose military vehicle. Production did not resume after the war.

The Willys was known for being "economical' and "nimble." The 1941-42 model was the last Willys car until 1952.

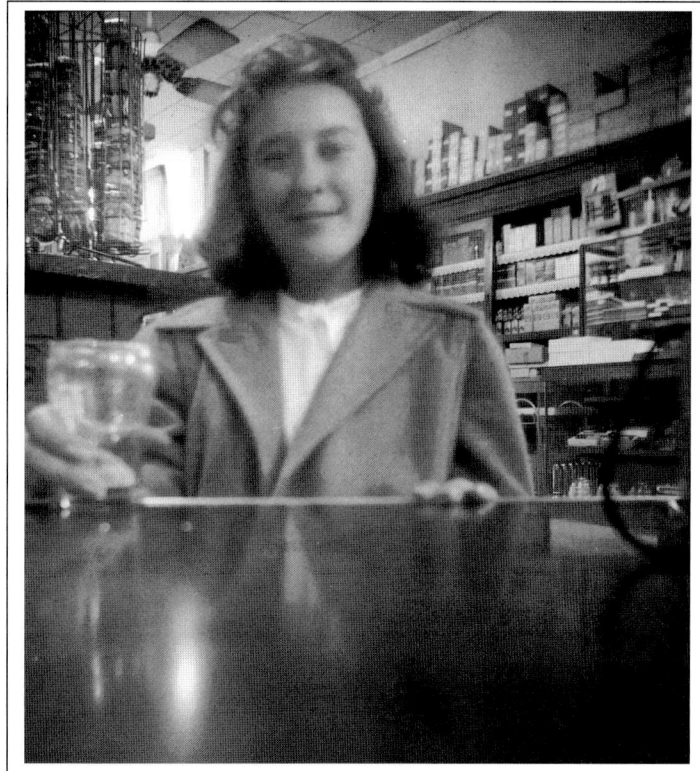

Louella Robinson enjoys a fountain Coke at Duncan Drug Store

The Soda Fountain —

During the 1940's and 1950's, small town and big city dwellers alike were able to enjoy "Coke," "Dr. Pepper," "Pepsi" and other carbonated beverages served in ice-cold glasses at a soda fountain or ice cream parlor — most often housed in a drugstore. The soda fountain offered custom-mixed drinks, along with other favorite menu items such as ice cream sodas, ice cream sundaes, malts and milkshakes, banana splits and some sandwiches. The soda fountain counters, as well as nearby booths and tables, were the meeting places for people of all ages, but most certainly for high school students after school or on dates.

The soft drinks were "mixed on the spot" by "soda jerks," mostly boys, who had a special slang language used for ordering those popular drinks. Although there might have been slight variations from fountain-to-fountain, for the most part, the soda fountain lingo seemed to be almost universal.

Soda fountain lingo was an interesting language. The "wild Waco," a Dr. Pepper cola with cherry syrup added, was a very popular soft drink. The "Waco" reference was for Waco, Texas, the city where the Dr. Pepper Company had its start and where the cola drink was developed. Coca-Cola, the most popular of soft drinks at the time, was originally developed in Atlanta, Georgia. That place of origin was the basis for creating such terms as "drag one through Georgia," for a Coca-Cola with chocolate added. Most "soda jerks" preferred the term "shot" for the Coke and "mud" for the chocolate, and "wild" for real cherry syrup flavoring. Thus, a "wild shot" would be an order for a cherry Coke.

These slang messages were perceived as a supposedly secret system of code names. Knowing the "lingo" made "Soda Jerks" feel very special since the customers, at least most of them, supposedly didn't know what those terms really meant and would be duly impressed. It is doubtful that customers were all that impressed.

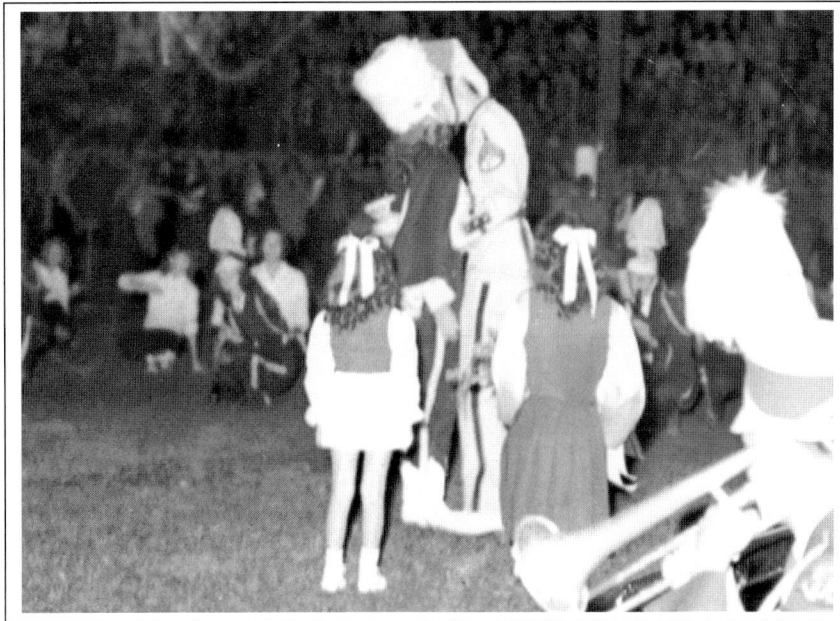

Crowning the Queen —
Drum Major Rusty Dunn "crowns" Band Queen Joy Rogers with kiss during football game
halftime ceremony. Photo was taken from the band's drum line while band continued to play.
— Fall 1946

Campus scene at Ada High School during noon break.
— Spring 1947

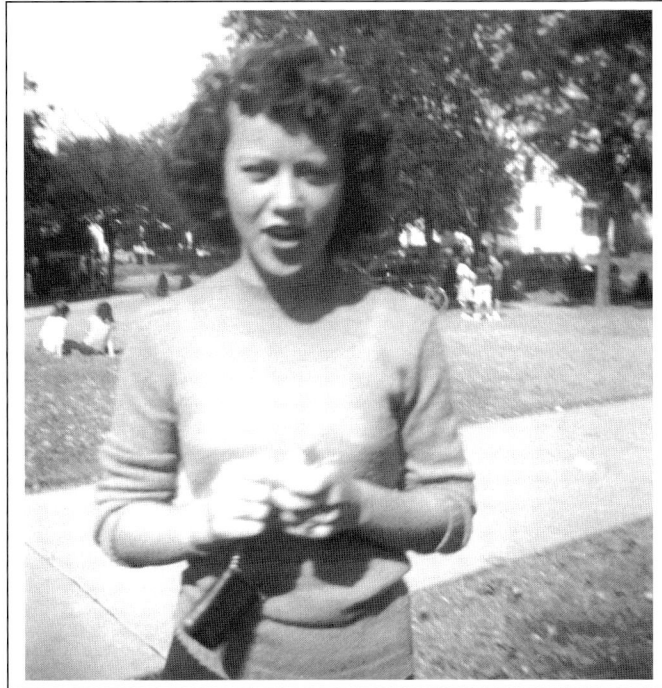

*High School Beauty —
Springtime weather provided
opportunities for high school
students to enjoy long lunchtime
breaks on the shady and grass-
covered Ada High School campus.
— Spring 1947*

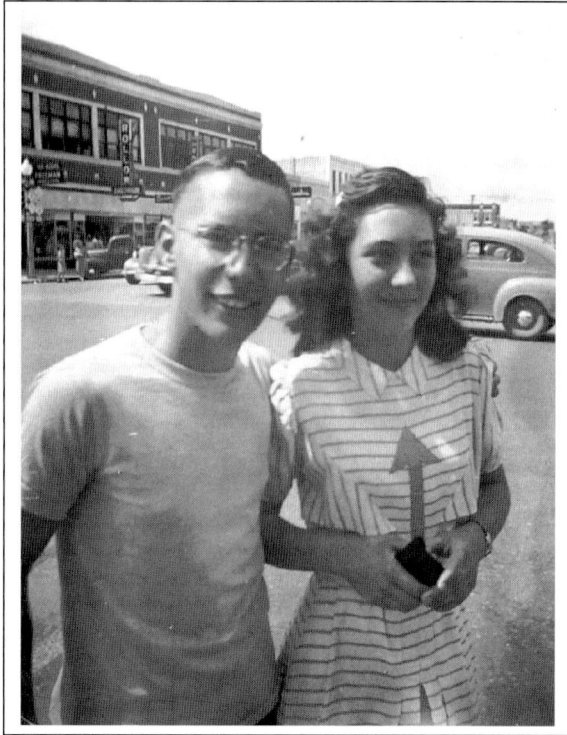

Enjoying Downtown —
Ben Floyd and Maxine Gulick
pause during a Springtime walk
on Main Street in downtown
Ada.

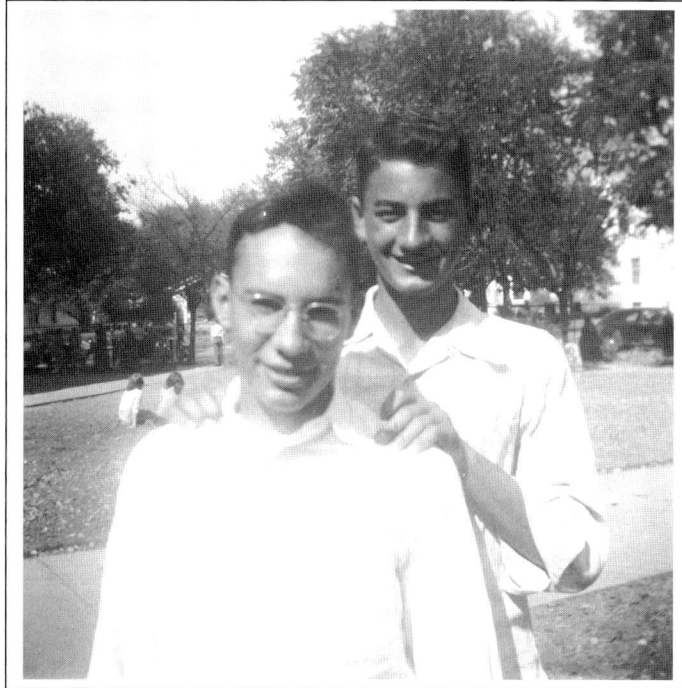

Friends for a lifetime —
Ben Floyd
and Clarence Oliver
on Ada High School campus.

The Hayride —
Young people are packed on the wagon for nighttime hayride.

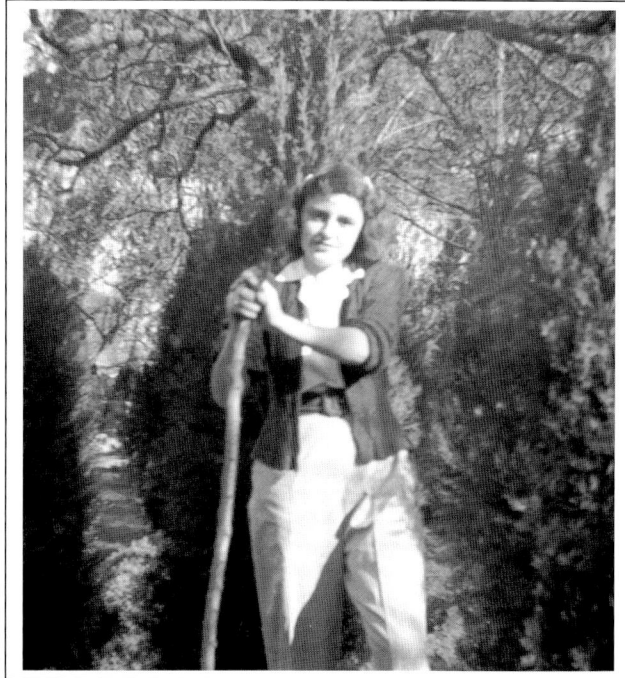

Ready for Hike —
Betty See, with trekking pole in
hand, enjoys climbing through the
"Rock Gardens" at East Central
College.

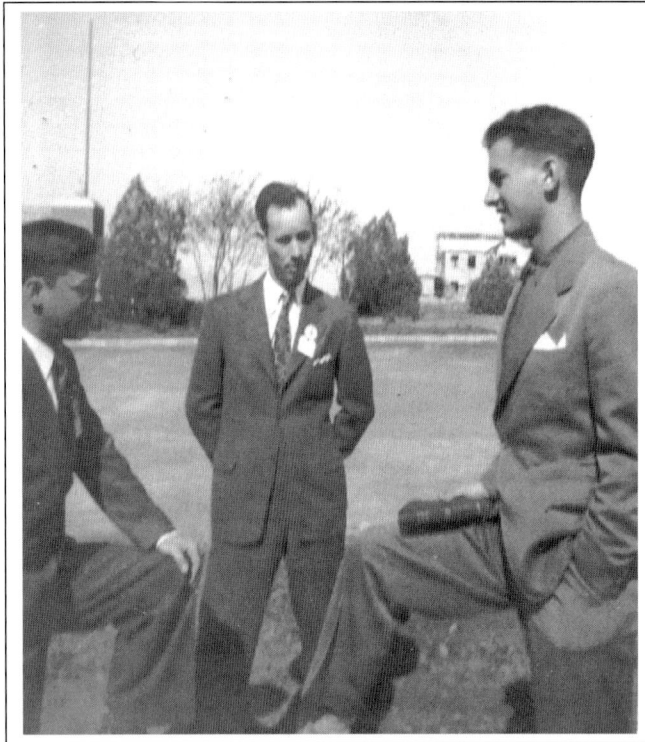

Serious Talk —
College students attending a
Bible conference on the campus
of Oklahoma Baptist
University, Shawnee,
Oklahoma, take a break
between conference sessions.

John Turley, left, another
conference participant, and
Clarence Oliver, right.
— Fall 1949

Students at a Baptist Student Union banquet, Oklahoma A&M College, Stillwater, Oklahoma. Vinita Shirley and Clarence Oliver, on right.
— 1949

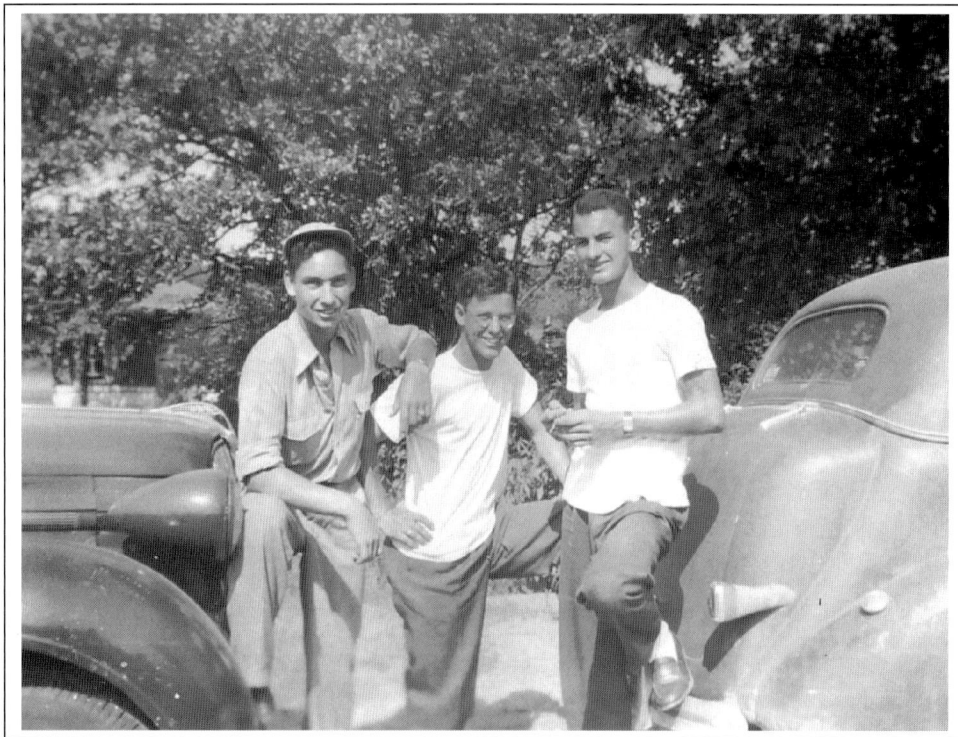

Guys just "Hanging out." —

Costume "Tacky" Party —
Students found ways to enjoy life by coming together for frequent parties. Friends gather at the Oliver home
for a "Tacky Party." Standing are Warren Mayfield, Betty Mitchell, Betty See, Vinita Shirley. Kneeling
are Bob Hudgens, Mary Nell Turley, Giles Mitchell.

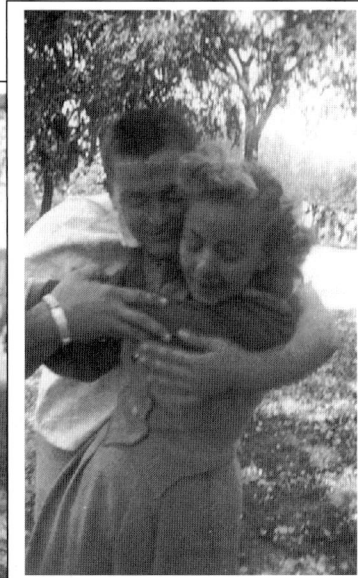

A little friendly "flirting" during noon break on Ada High School campus. E. A. Guinn and Jaxine Yeagle

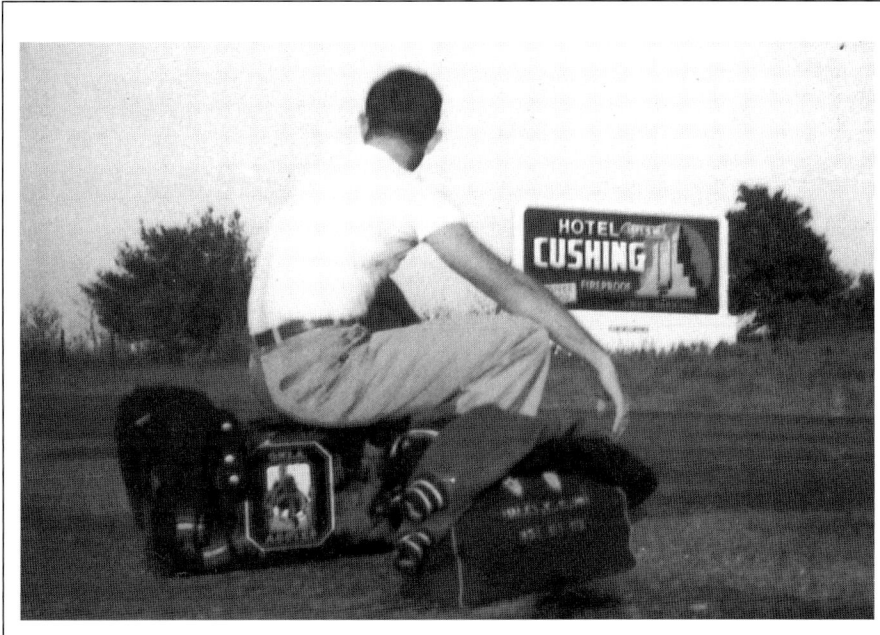

The Hitchhiker —
Hitchhiking home to Ada from Oklahoma A&M College in Stillwater was a standard way to travel for young college students with limited income and who did not own a car. Ed Haley sits at the side of the highway near Cushing, Oklahoma, "thumbin'" for a ride and patiently waiting for a willing driver to stop and offer a ride—at least to the next town or highway connection.

Nighttime scenes on campus of Oklahoma A&M College, Stillwater, Oklahoma.
— Fall 1949

Amateur Astronomers—
Ed Haley stands with the telescope that he and Clarence Oliver made. The telescope provided hours of enjoyment for the two students—as well as friends and neighbors. The Oliver's 1934 Plymouth sedan, with front opening "suicide doors," is parked in front of the Oliver home where the telescope was often in use each night, weather permitting.

— Fall 1948

Homemade Telescope —

An early interest in Astronomy, sparked by college science classes, gave Clarence Oliver and Ed Haley a desire to own a high-powered telescope so they could study the moon, planets and stars. Since money was not available for them to purchase a quality instrument, they decided to build one. Through a contact found in a science magazine advertisement, they ordered sets of ground lenses from an optical firm in Germany, and a few weeks later they had in hand the most critical component of the planned telescope.

The focal lengths of the various lenses were carefully calculated—and the work began. A six-foot long heavy-duty cylinder that had been used to hold a roll of linoleum flooring was obtained from a furniture store for the telescope's main tube. A smaller cylinder was located to serve as the eyepiece. Mounting rings to hold lenses in place were carefully hand cut and placed inside the cylinders. The lenses were installed in the eyepiece and the larger cylinder. A six-feet tall metal base, with a mounting bracket to hold the telescope, was designed, the needed pieces of scrap iron and steel pipe were purchased from a scrap metal dealer, and a hometown welder was contracted to weld the base together. The base and cylinders were hand painted with black enamel paint.

A search through the stacks of surplus World War II items in an Army surplus store uncovered precision parts of a bombsight that could be used to make minute adjustments for minor directional changes of the telescope. The set of lenses could be changed to provide magnification up to 500-power—permitting the amateur astronomers the opportunity to study the rings of Saturn, the many moons of Jupiter, see the Earth's moon up close, to check on the closer planets of Venice and Mars and study the various star constellations.

Friends and neighbors frequently showed up in the Oliver's front yard to try out the "neighborhood telescope." When Clarence Oliver left for active military duty at the start of the Korean War in July 1950, the telescope was given to one of the young boys living in the neighborhood.

Girlfriends on Outing —
College friends frequently found
brief respite from classes by going
to nearby Wintersmith Park for
lunch and a time of relaxation.

Such outings occurred during all
seasons, even if the picnic
required wearing winter coats in
order to enjoy the winter
sunlight.

Little Girls at Heart —
Eighteen or nineteen years of age is a good time in life. Young ladies can still enjoy remembering carefree childhood days, as did these college students on a winter's day outing at Wintersmith Park in 1949.

College Friends —
Betty See. Bernice Miller, unidentified, Vinita Shirley and Maxine Kem

Football Stars —
Glen McGinnis, starting tackle, and J. R. Johnson, outstanding running back for the Ada High
School Cougars, on sidelines during football practice. Men in suits watch the team practice.

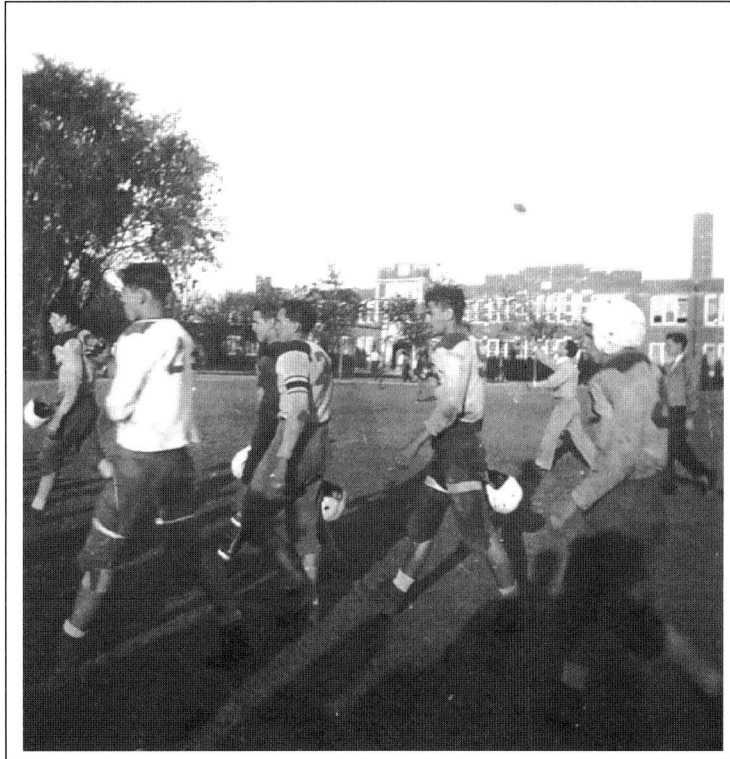

Half-Time —
Ada High School football
players head to the locker
room at half-time in a game
between Ada and Pauls
Valley High Schools on
November 11,1946.

Players wore canvas pant,
heavy leather shoes, and
leather helmets without face
guards

High School Buddies —
E. A. Guinn
and Bob Overstreet
visit in the Oliver's home.

Large "ash tray" stands,
similar to the stand in the
lower right portion of the
photograph, were common
furnishings in most homes.

A Great Start—
A split second makes the difference in a good start as these runners speed from the "blocks," the small indentures dug into the cinder track surface, in the 100-yard dash competition at a regional track meet held at Norris field track in Spring 1948

The "High Hurdles" —
Runners clear the first hurdles in the 110-yard high hurdles race during regional track competition at the Norris Field track in Ada in Spring 1948.

Baton Exchange —
Last lap of one-mile relay race. Spectators watch intently as runners make the critical
baton exchange.

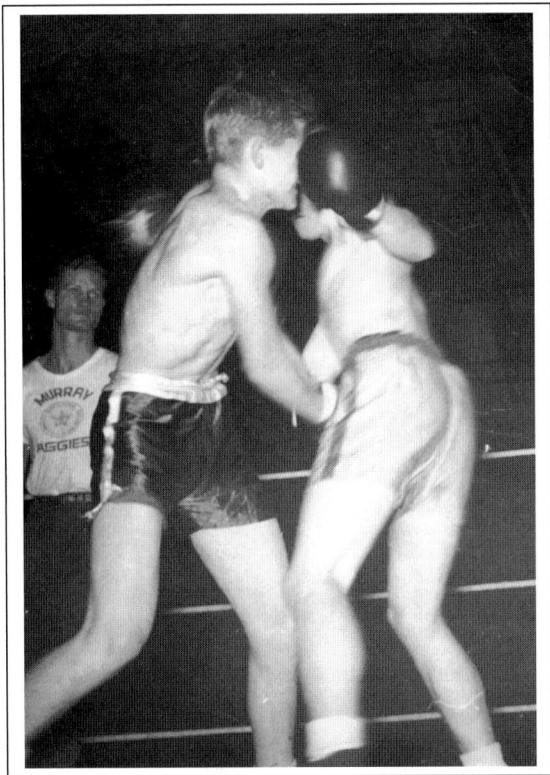

Golden Gloves Boxing —

Amateur boxing flourished in Oklahoma during the 1940's and 1950's, and was a popular activity at Oklahoma's high schools, colleges and universities, and military installations.

Ada's Golden Gloves events, such as this lightweight match, were held in the National Guard Armory and attracted large crowds.

The Oklahoma Golden Gloves tournament of 1946 in Oklahoma City attracted more than 20,000 spectators. Boxers from 49 Oklahoma communities, including Ada, competed in the 1949 state tournament. The Oklahoma squad won the national Golden Gloves team title in 1949.

Track team practice at Oklahoma A&M College Spring 1950

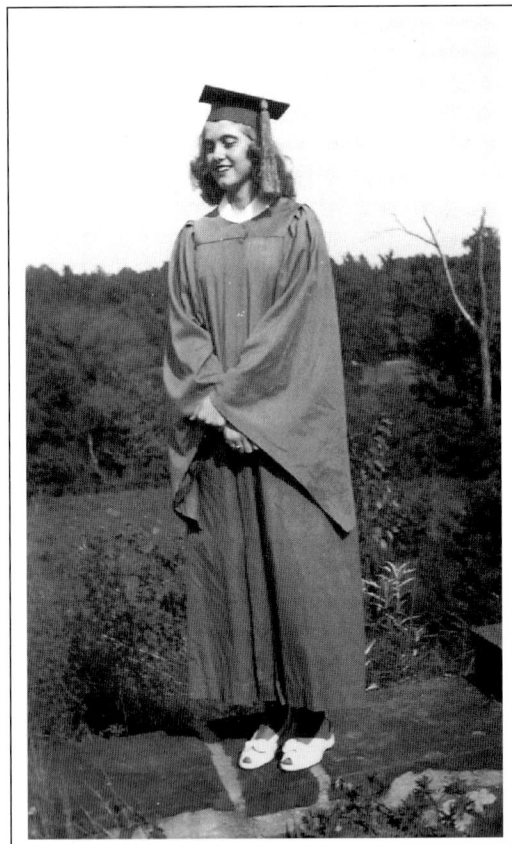

Graduation Time —
Vinita June Shirley in mortarboard and
gown on Baccalaureate Sunday, May 1948.

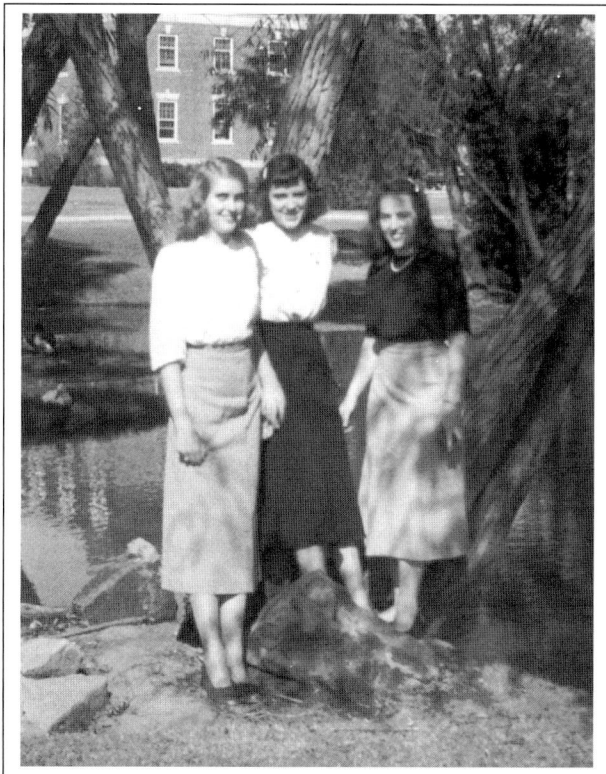

At Theta Pond —
Vinita Shirley, Betty See and
Mary Nell Turley on campus at
Oklahoma A&M College,
Stillwater, Oklahoma.
— Fall 1949

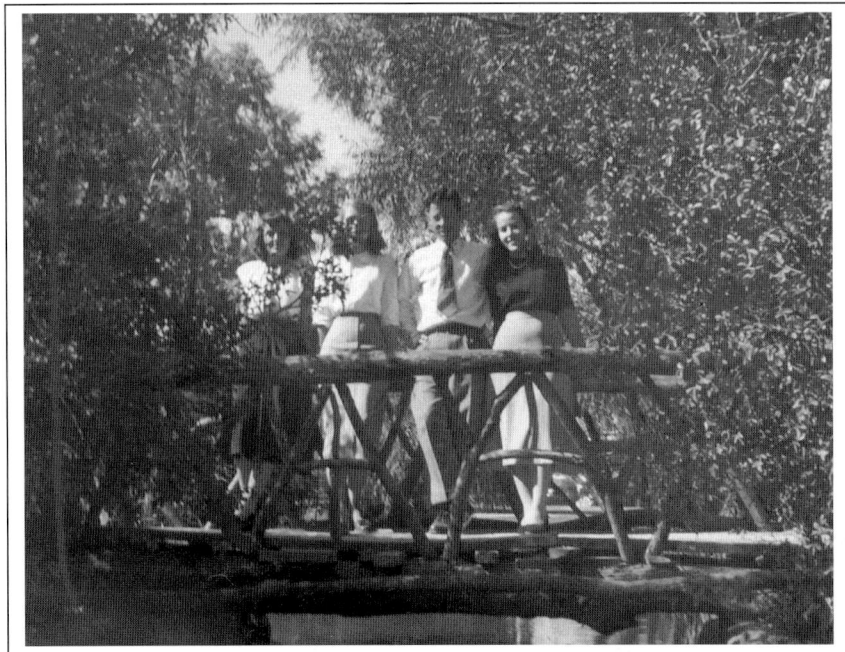

Homecoming Day, 1949 —
Betty See, Vinita Shirley, John Turley and Mary Nell Turley on a bridge at Theta Pond on
campus of Oklahoma A&M College, Stillwater, Oklahoma.

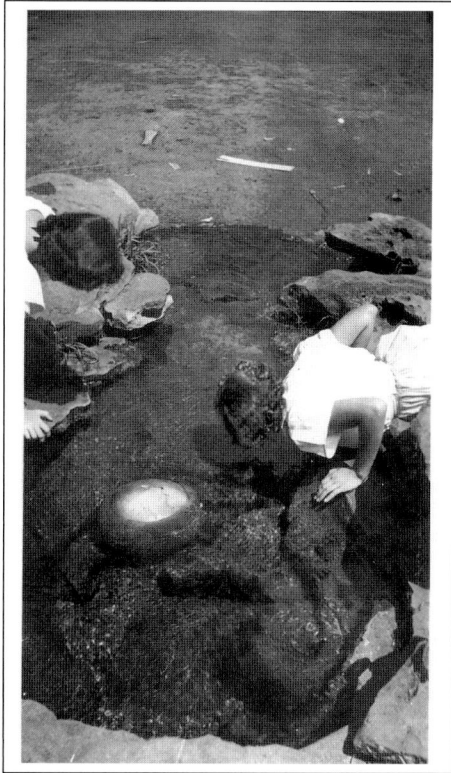

Sparkling Spring Water —

Fresh spring water constantly flowed into the 15-acre Wintersmith Park Lake, once the city's water supply. Park visitors could drink the cold spring water by kneeling and filling cups or just sipping directly from the source.

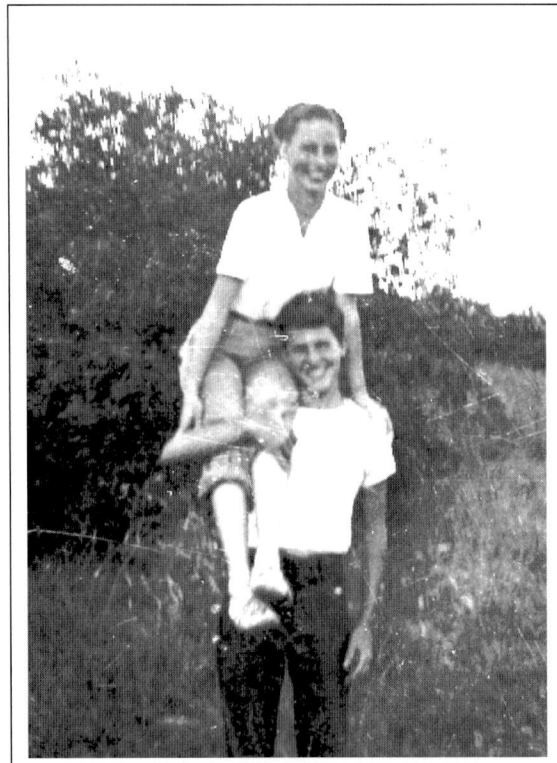

Junior-Senior Picnic —
Glen Wood performs a "Charles
Atlas" like act by lifting Billie
Jean Fathree onto his shoulder at
the Ada High School Class
picnic.
          — May 1947

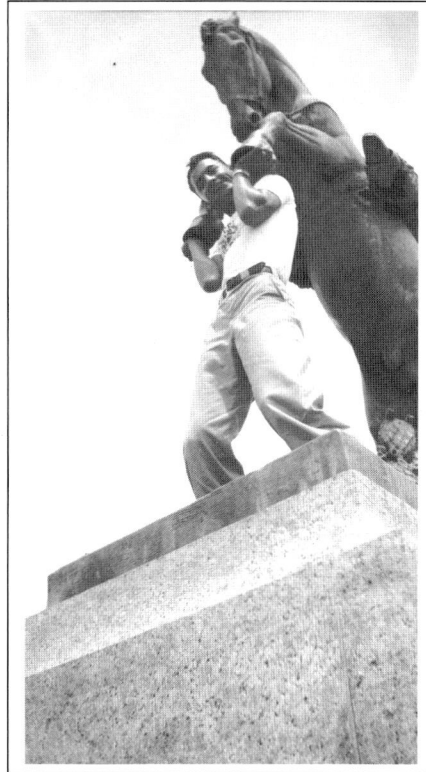

"Horsing Around" —
Clarence Oliver "clowns" a bit with a
horse statue in front of the Oklahoma
State Capitol.
                    — July 4, 1949

The *"Big Dipper" at Springlake Amusement Park, Oklahoma City*

View from top of Big Dipper — Oil derricks on the horizon. Oklahoma City, Oklahoma.
— Summer 1949

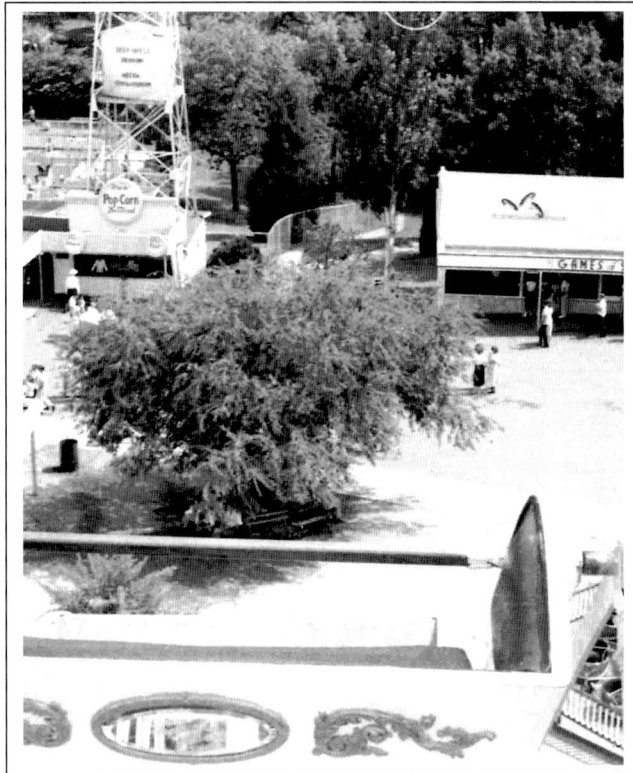

View from the top of the Ferris Wheel, Springlake Amusement Park, Oklahoma City.

Oklahoma's First TV Tower —

The State's first Television tower was erected on the
northern edge of Oklahoma City for use by WKY-
TV, Channel 4, and was about 900 feet tall. The
station went "on-the-air" on June 6, 1949.

TV was in its infancy. The station broadcast only a
few hours each day. When the station was off the air,
sometimes people just sat and stared at the test pattern,
and marveled at how the little box with a window in
the front of it could snatch moving black and white
pictures and sound out of the air (through an antenna
on the roof) and allow people to view them at home in
the living room.

— July 4, 1949

Start of Television in Oklahoma —

The young people in "the Gang" loaded into two cars, the Oliver's 1938 Chevrolet sedan and the Marshall's 1937 Chevrolet sedan, on July 4, 1949, for a one-day outing to "see the sights" in Oklahoma City—especially the first television tower in Oklahoma. The tower had been completed just one month earlier. None of the families owned one of the new television sets, but the college students had heard of the innovative new technology and wanted to see the historical site of the state's first TV tower.

The new means of communications came on the scene in the late 1930s. In November 1939 RCA (Radio Corporation of America) conducted a WKY-sponsored demonstration of the new medium in the new Oklahoma City Municipal Auditorium. Edward K. Gaylord, owner of the Oklahoma Publishing Company and the state's premier daily newspaper, *The Daily Oklahoman,* and WKY radio station, promised to make television available in Oklahoma as soon as possible. World War II slowed progress, but true to Gaylord's word, WKY-TV went on the air in June 1949. It was the state's first television station.

The station signed on the air on June 6, 1949, as WKY-TV, Channel 4, and took a primary affiliation with NBC due to WKY radio's association with NBC Radio. The station's original studios were located at the Municipal Auditorium in downtown Oklahoma City, with local programming broadcast from the Little Theatre. A few months later, on October 22, 1949, KOTV, Channel 6, became the first Tulsa station to begin on-air programming. At the time, there were only 90 TV stations in the country, with fewer than 10 west of the Mississippi

The first shows were crude. Live programming came from local station studios and the national programs were supplied by kinescope—taped recordings—rushed to the station by airplane with a minimum delay of about a week between productions and broadcast. The newfangled TV sets were nearly an instant hit, in spite of the expense. Most TVs with 10- or 12-1/2-inch screens cost more than $800—a significant amount in 1949 dollars. Everyone had black-and-white sets, but color was the talk of the day.

The Way We Were —
During those days we call "A Time of Peace, Season of Innocence."

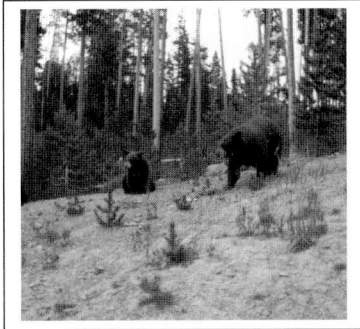

Chapter Seven

Great Western Adventure —

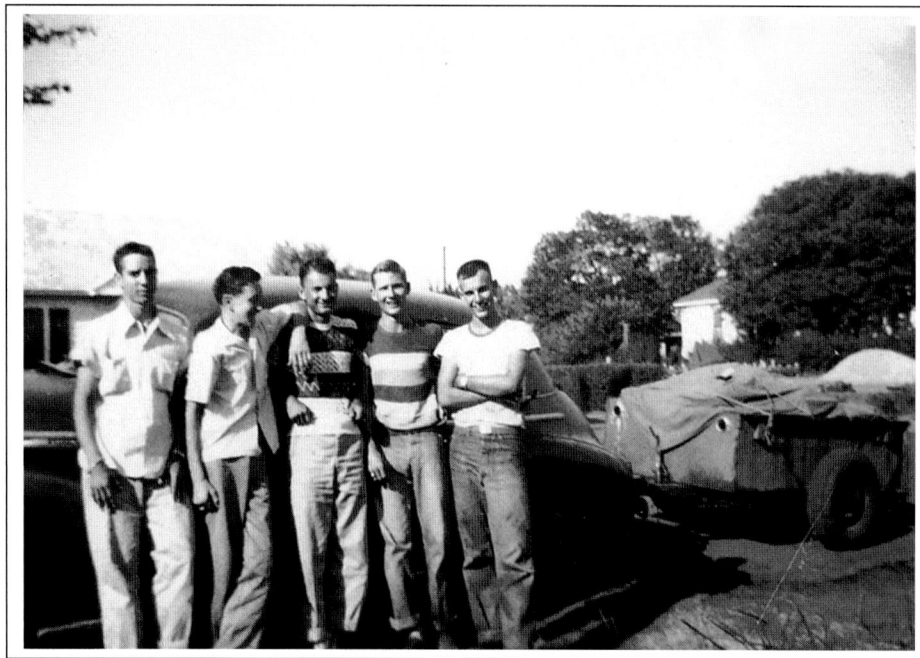

The Morning of Departure —
Five buddies pose in front of car and trailer as they leave on a two-week long driving and camping trip through eight western states—an adventure remembered for a lifetime. Left to right: Bill Williams, Kenneth Watson, Clarence Oliver, Dale Dawson, Robert (Bob) Hudgens.

Crossing the border into Texas

Low Budget Vacation Trip —

Not many young people, at least those from average families in small-town Ada, Oklahoma, had opportunities for vacation trips during the 1940s. During the summer of 1948, five buddies—recent Ada High School graduates—decided to make a multi-state, two-week long driving and camping trip through western Oklahoma, West Texas, New Mexico, Colorado, Wyoming, Montana, Idaho and Utah.

A well-used 1941 Chevrolet sedan was made available through the generosity of Bob Hudgen's father, who owned a Nash automobile dealership. An old two-wheel trailer was borrowed to transport all the gear—a canvas tent, Coleman stove, Coleman lanterns, cots, blankets or sleeping bags, food supplies and spare clothing.

This was a great adventure—one remembered for a lifetime.

Colorado River view, with railroad running along the riverbank.

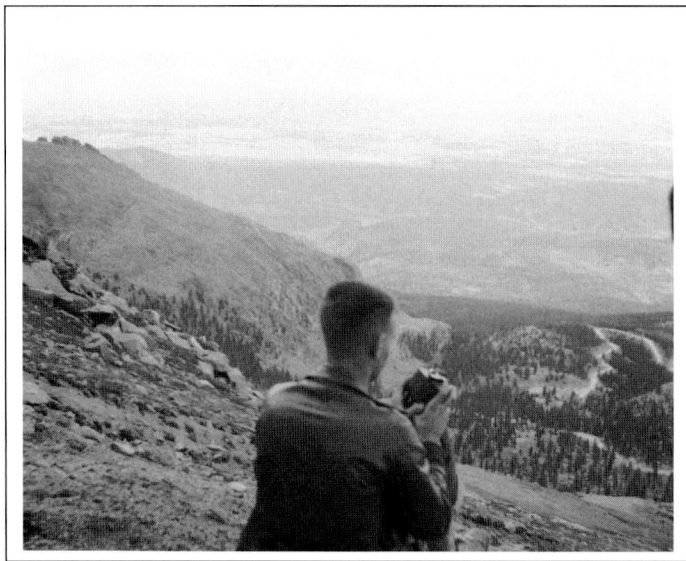

The mountains and valleys of the Rocky Mountains were awe-inspiring.

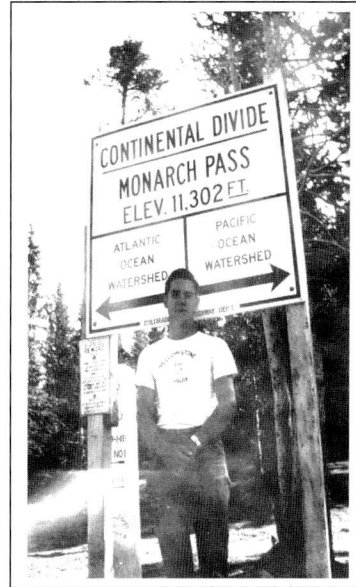

Bill at Monarch Pass

Driving through a tunnel in "the Rockies" was a new experience for young Oklahomans—as was crossing the "Continental Divide."

Rocky Mountain peak—in northern New Mexico

Natural Bridge in the
"Rockies"

Bears in Yellowstone Park —
Living with free-roaming bears was a new
experience for the boys from Oklahoma.

A campsite was established in
Yellowstone National Park for two or
three days, with a plan to explore all
areas of the park in short day trips.

Upon returning to the campsite on the
first evening, the "explorers" discovered
that the bears—who also left the tent,
cots and equipment in disarray—had
enjoyed much of the food left at camp.

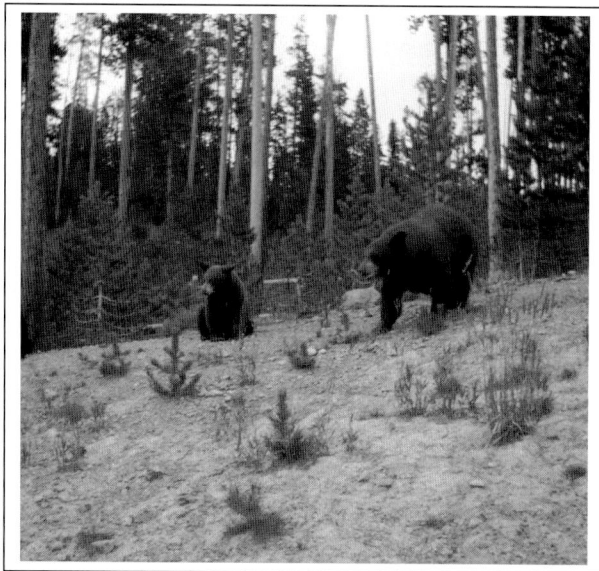

The Roosevelt Arch —

The Roosevelt Arch near Gardiner, Montana, marks the North Entrance to Yellowstone National Park. This stone arch was designed by Robert Reamer (who also designed the Old Faithful Inn) and built in 1903. President Theodore Roosevelt positioned the mortar upon which the large cornerstone was set, and the arch took on his name. The inscription above the arch says, "For the benefit and enjoyment of the people," which was taken directly from a speech he made on April 24, 1903. The words were written in the Yellowstone National Park Act of 1872 that created Yellowstone National Park, America's first National Park. In the early 1900s, visitors would arrive by train in Gardiner, and take stagecoaches through this entrance into the Park. Automobiles were not allowed into the Park for many years, as it was thought they would frighten the horses pulling the stagecoaches through the Park.

"The Yellowstone Park is something absolutely unique in the world . . . This Park was created and is now administered for the benefit and enjoyment of the people . . . it is the property of Uncle Sam and therefore of us all."

> — President Theodore Roosevelt
> April 24, 1903, at Gardiner, Montana
> Speech dedicating the North Entrance Arch

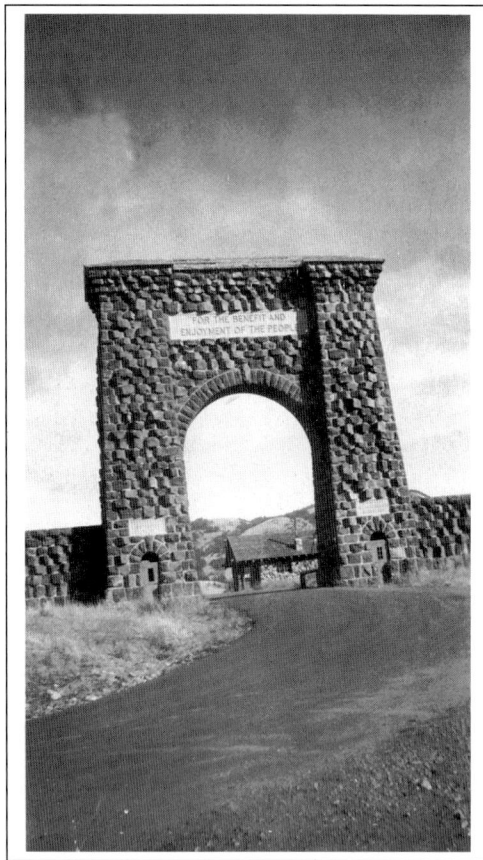

The North entrance to Yellowstone
National Park, near Gardiner, Montana

Yellowstone River in Yellowstone National Park, Wyoming

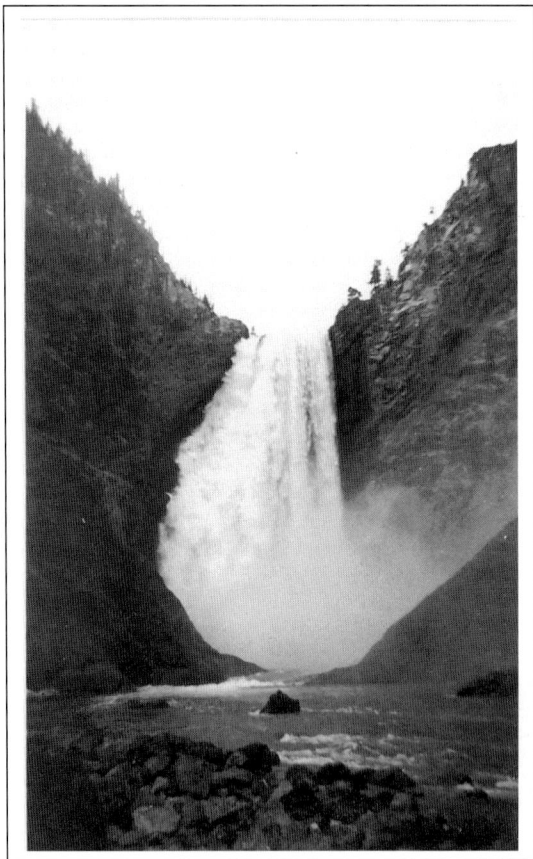

Upper falls of Yellowstone River in Yellowstone National Park.

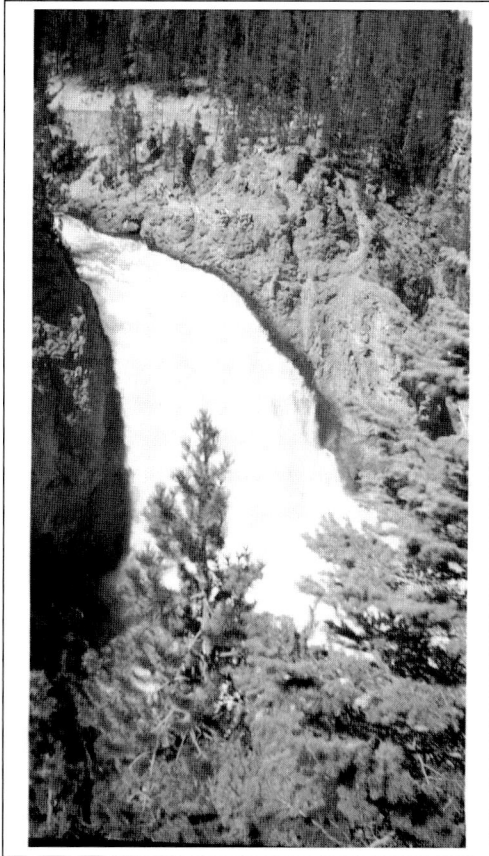

Lower Falls of Yellowstone River
in Yellowstone National Park.

Mammoth Hot Springs in
Yellowstone National Park

Pike's Peal—from a distance—and the majestic nearby Rocky Mountains

Campsite on side of Pikes Peak

Early Morning on Pike's Peak —

A campsite was set up high on the side of Pikes Peak. The five young men discussed "climbing to the top" of the mountain from the campsite, but after a short distance of that effort, the group decided the "climb" might be a bit more difficult that it appeared. The driving trip to the top was made the following day. The trip down was almost a disaster.

The Majestic Rocky Mountains in Colorado —
A major mountain range in western North America, "the Rockies" stretch almost 3,000 miles from
the northernmost part of British Columbia, in western Canada, to New Mexico. The range's highest
peak is Mount Elbert, located in Colorado at 14,400 feet above sea level. The most visited mountain
in North America, though, is Pikes Peak, with an altitude of 14,110 feet above sea level.

A Disaster Avoided —

The harrowing trip down from the top of Pikes Peak was an unforgettable experience—one that was almost a deadly disaster. For most of the two-weeks of driving, the car's fuel gauge frequently was at a point closer to "Empty" than "Full." The travelers were watching every penny in the carefully calculated fuel budget—always looking for a station with the cheapest gasoline. The drive "up" Pikes Peak consumed more fuel than the "flat-land" boys from Oklahoma had anticipated.

Shortly after beginning the drive down the mountain, the engine "coughed" and the fuel gauge rested on "E." The engine "died" just as the driver, Bob Hudgens, moved the gearshift lever into neutral, planning to restart the engine with a "jump start" in a lower gear while the car moved down the narrow mountain road. They were about the 10,000-foot elevation level on the 14,100-foot mountain. The mountain highway ran 20 miles from the entry point. The "bottom" was miles away—and nothing but a narrow, steep, winding road ahead.

The Chevrolet cars of the early 1940s—including the 1941 sedan being used on this trip—were proudly advertised in newspapers and magazines as a car that featured a 90 horsepower engine, body by Fisher, with "vacuum" power shift, and "tiptoe-matic" clutch. The transmission was a manual synchromesh three-speed, with vacuum assisted shift, in which the "three-on-the-tree" shifter moved between gears by the slightest pressure on the lever. The car also featured hydraulic brakes with all-wheel drums.

A Disaster Avoided (Continued) —

The vacuum shift was nice, except, as learned in a split second on the mountain, the engine had to be running to produce the vacuum to permit gears to be shifted. No fuel, no engine, no vacuum. The car was in neutral—speeding down the narrow, curving mountain road at 50 or 60 miles per hour. The driver hit the brakes again and again, eventually with full-time pressure on the brakes. The brake shoes smoked and screamed.

The wild ride down ended just as the brakes disintegrated and screeching sounds came from the drums on all wheels.

Among the signs at the top of the mountain with instructions to drivers was one that read, "Use your lowest gear to allow your engine to brake your vehicle. Don't ride your brakes. This will cause them to overheat and cause problems."

Truer words were never written!

Pikes Peak — on the "drive up"

Adventure-filled Trip —

The five travelers set up the tent and camping equipment along roadsides in Texas and New Mexico, camped without permission in city parks in Hot Springs, New Mexico; Cody, Wyoming, and Manitou Springs, Colorado; picked up "General Delivery" mail held at the post office in Casper, Wyoming, and camped along the highways in Wyoming and Idaho. On a couple of occasions, city police stopped to inquire, "what is going on?" — but decided to overlook the fact that no one gave permission for the overnight camping. Most of the breakfast and "supper" meals were prepared at the campsite. Lunch, if obtained, most often was hamburgers, fries and milkshakes at some small restaurant along the way.

The car ran out of gasoline on a nighttime drive in the mountains in southeastern Idaho. The five decided to use an "alternative fuel" and poured in a gallon of white gasoline that was carried for the camping stove and lanterns to get enough fuel to drive another 10-12 miles. The gasoline tank was drained dry. With one person behind the wheel, the other four pushed the car and trailer up a mountain and coasted in to St. Charles, Idaho, about daylight the following day.

When a service station opened for business, the tank was filled, the carburetor primed to start the engine—and the travelers headed south to Utah.

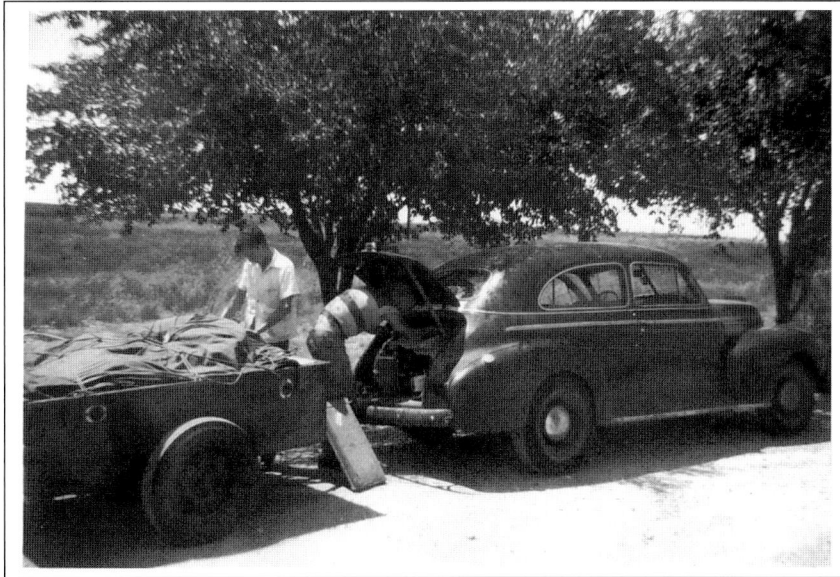

Repacking the trailer and trunk after camping overnight along a highway in northeastern in New Mexico.

Last Leg Home —

The days in the Pikes Peak area of central and then eastern Colorado were to be the last part of the two-week trip. The "adventurers" had crossed through much of central and western Colorado several days earlier on the way to Jackson Hole, Yellowstone National Park, Wyoming, Montana, Idaho and Utah. The last leg home from Colorado Springs would take two days. The trip "budget" did not include money to repair the car. Individual cash was getting low. The five boys pooled money, the car was pushed into a garage in Manitou Springs, Colorado, at the foot of Pike's Peak, and a complete "brake job" was obtained. The "Pikes Peak or Bust" slogan used by the people who made the1859 Gold Rush to Colorado took on a new meaning to the five young Oklahomans. "Bust" was a good description of their financial status.

The travelers were about 800 miles from home. The money that had been placed in the fund to buy fuel and food had been used. After the brake repair costs were paid, none of the five had much individual money left. They talked about "hiring out" as day laborer "pickers" for some of the many Cherry orchards in the area, trying to earn enough money for the final two days of the trip. Those jobs were already filled.

After much discussion, they decided to eat very little, to use the last of the canned food that had been purchased for the camping stops, and try to keep enough money to purchase gasoline.

The five arrived home "broke," absolutely without money, having pooled all the remaining cash (all coins, something less than $2.00) to purchase gasoline for the final 90 miles of the trip from Oklahoma City to Ada.

The great western adventure was over—but never forgotten.

The five "Amigos"

Chapter Eight

Early Military Days —

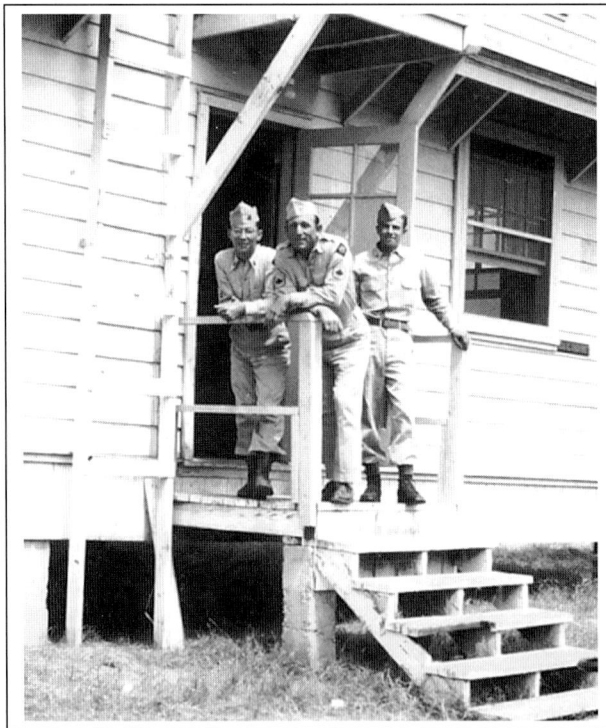

The Fort Sill Experience —

Sergeant Benny Floyd, (left),
First Sergeant Eugene (Doonie)
Alford, and Private Delbert
Marshall on porch of barracks at
Fort Sill, Oklahoma.
— August 1948

Wearing Army Khaki and Green —

The accomplishments of Oklahoma's famous 45th Infantry Division were well known to young men in Ada, Oklahoma. Many fathers, brothers, uncles and cousins had served as "Thunderbirds" during World War II.

When the effort to organize the Oklahoma National Guard's post-war 45th Infantry Division began, many of Ada's young men "signed up" with the hopes of being part-time soldiers, earning some extra money for the weekly drills and summer field training. Oliver and several friends "joined up" with the intent of using the extra money to help pay college tuition.

First Duty —
The first summer military training for brand
new Private Clarence Oliver and other high
school friends who joined the newly
reorganized 45th Infantry Division was in
August 1947 at Fort Sill, Oklahoma.
Oliver is pictured outside barracks with
combat pack and rifle, preparing for cross-
country field march.

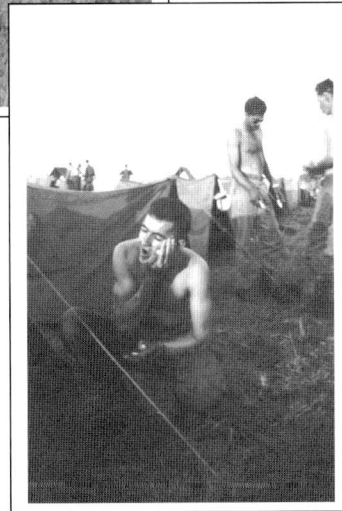

The Bivouac —
The grass-covered plains of Fort Sill in western Oklahoma
became a "pup tent city" when the scores of two-man tents
were set up in a bivouac area following cross-country field
march. Private Oliver prepares for early morning start, using
inverted steel helmet for bathing and shaving.
— August 1947

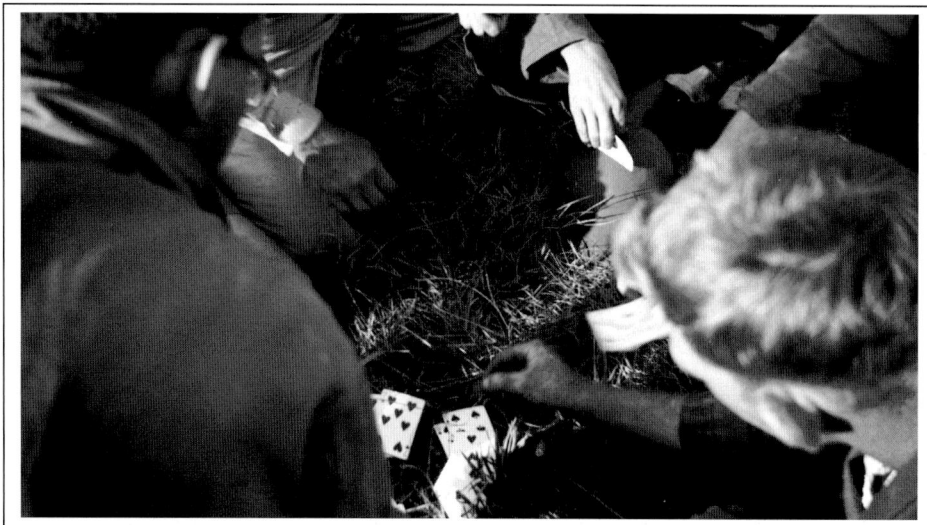

Card Game by Flashlight —
Benny Floyd, Carlos "Pinky" Ryan and others enjoy a nighttime card game of "Hearts," using flashlights for illumination, during Bivouac at Fort Sill, Oklahoma.
— August 1947

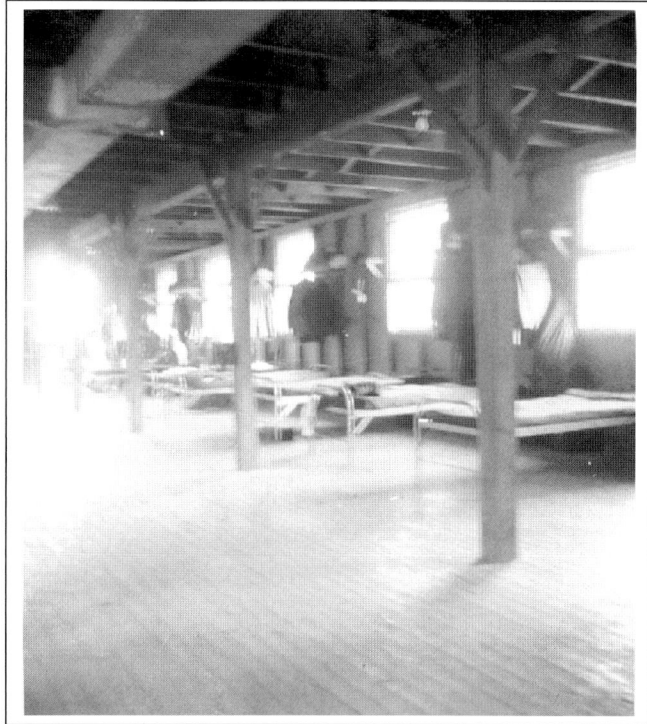

Barracks at
Fort Sill, Oklahoma,
August 1947

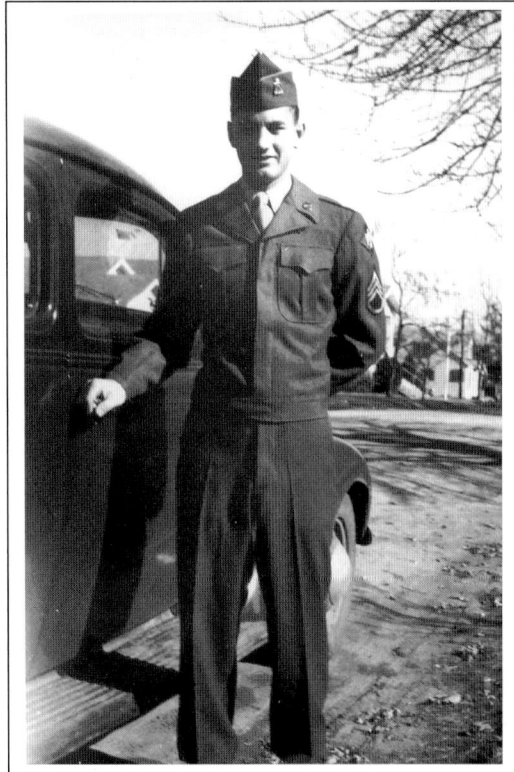

Honor Guard for WWII Dead —

Approximately 6,000 servicemen from Oklahoma, including 120 from Pontotoc County, died in World War II battles. Their bodies in flag-covered caskets were returned home during the 1946, 1947, 1948 years, and the young National Guardsmen from Ada who were serving in the 45ᵗʰ Infantry Division were called on to provide Honor Guards for the burial of many of those veterans.

Sergeant Oliver leaving home to serve on an Honor Guard detail for a "fallen hero" of Word War II.

The 45ᵗʰ Infantry Division Championship Rifle Team —
Warrant Officer Paul Alford, Corporal C. Kidd, Sergeant Clarence Oliver and
Sergeant Richard Bell are pictured during the rifle team competition. Alford and
Bell were World War II veterans.

— 1948

Championship
Medal —

The Championship Rifle Team —

Earning a spot as a member of the Company C, 180th Infantry Regiment, Rifle Team was a personal goal of the new Sergeant Oliver. Two teams were selected for the company and Oliver was named to the unit's "second team." The teams were entered in the 45th Division state championship rifle competition held at a rifle range near Durant, Oklahoma. The expert marksmen from all units from across Oklahoma competed throughout the day.

The marksmen were armed with standard Garand M1 .30 caliber rifles, and fired a specified number of rounds from the 200, 300 and 500 yard ranges, in the standing, kneeling, sitting and prone positions from each specified distance, and being scored for both slow fire and rapid fire action.

When scores were tallied at the end of the day, Company C's "second team" was declared the winning team — the Division's best riflemen. Two years later, with the start of the Korean War, the marksmanship skills would prove very useful.

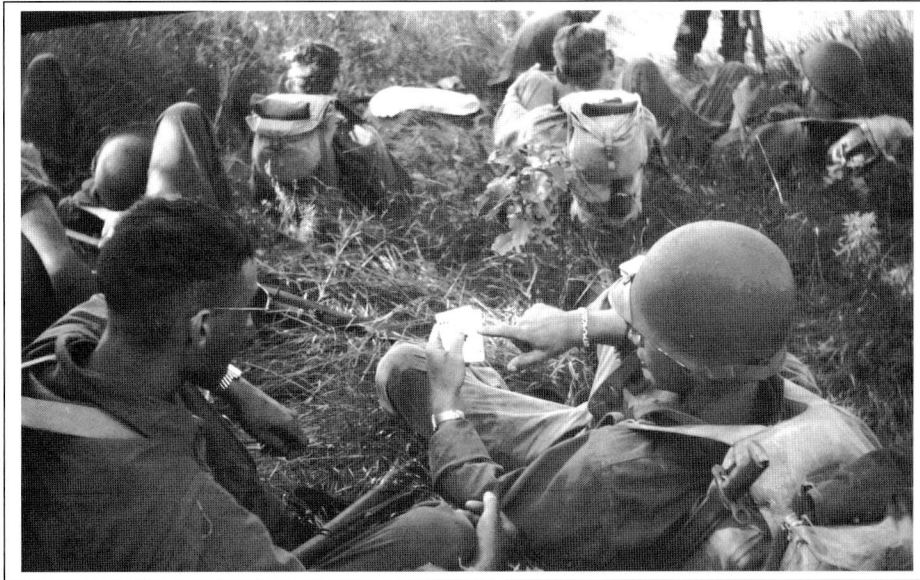

Ten-minute break during long field march with full combat packs and rifles. The short rest breaks came every hour when soldiers made long cross-country field marches. Privates Benny Floyd and Clarence Oliver talk about maybe playing a game of "Hearts."
— *Fort Sill, Oklahoma, August 1947*

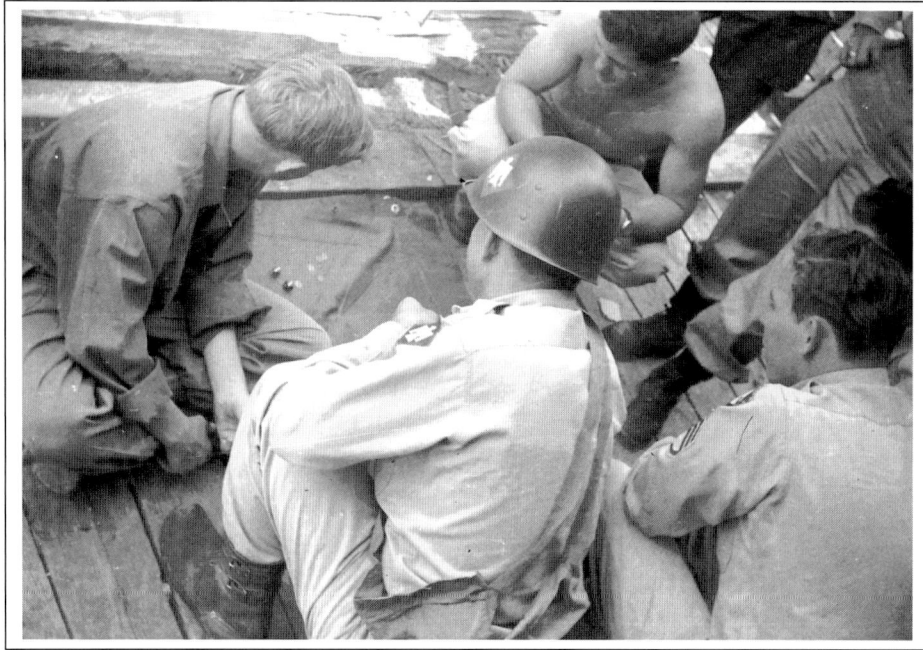

Roll the Dice —
A break-time game of street "Craps" remained a trivial "penny ante" game with the unit's
commanding officer looking over the shoulders of players. A canvas pup tent half was unrolled to create
an informal game table for soldiers on "pit duty" at the rifle range on the former Ardmore Army Air
Base, near Gene Autry, Oklahoma.

Checking for Ticks —
Anyone spending time walking, training and camping in the grassy, brush or woodland areas of
Oklahoma during summer months knew to make "tick checks" several times a day to look for the
annoying small nymph "seed ticks." After lying on the ground at the rifle range, this "shooter" found
that ticks around his waist required immediate attention for a bit of first aid. The "tick search"
brought some friendly "support" and advice from other shooters. Rifle range scene on the former
Ardmore Army Air Base, near Gene Autry, Oklahoma.

—Summer 1948

Lt. Dominic Vietta was officer on duty in "the pits" at the rifle range. Since no visitors could "drop in" to the pit area—the receiving end of rifle fire—the officer on duty decided to "grab some nap time." Lt. Vietta previously served in the U.S. Marine Corps during World War II. Rifle range on the former Ardmore Army Air Base, near Gene Autry, Oklahoma.

— Summer 1948

Tent City —
Setting up pup tents in
bivouac area on the
former Ardmore Army
Air Base, near Gene
Autry, Oklahoma.
— Summer 1948

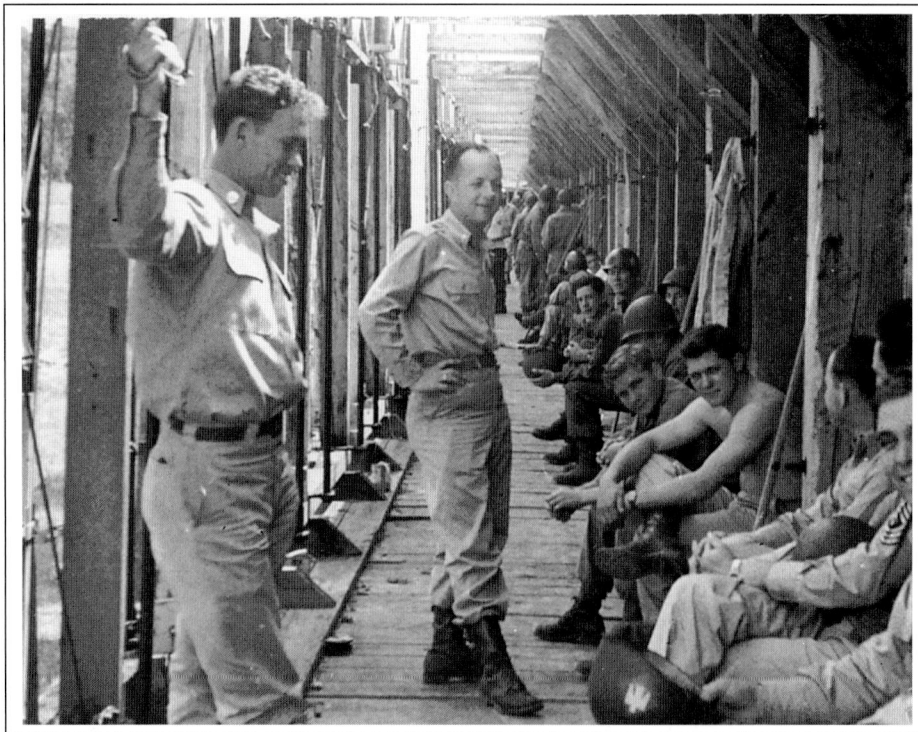

Rifle Range Pit Duty —
Sergeant Richard Bell, left, and Captain Craig McBroom, company commander, chat with
soldiers on "pit duty" at rifle range on the former Ardmore Army Air Base, near Gene Autry,
Oklahoma.

— Summer 1948

The Army Rifle Range and the "Pits" —

A typical Army Rifle Range during the post-World War II era had 20 to 30 firing points, raised slightly higher than nearby ground. Firing lines were located at 100-yards, 300-yards, and 500-yards from the target pits. The soldiers were armed with the Garand M1 .30 caliber rifle, and fired a specified number of rounds from the 100, 300 and 500 yard lines, in the standing, kneeling, sitting and prone positions from each specified distance, and were scored for both slow fire and rapid fire action.

The target pits were a partially covered concrete walkway and bench area behind a concrete wall and heavy earthen berm. The top of the berm was approximately eight feet higher than the catwalk. At the back of the catwalk and berm area were large frame target carriers, with an impact berm behind the targets to absorb the thousands of lead bullets fired at targets. Each carrier held a target frame of approximately five-feet square in size that held paper bull's-eye targets.

In an organized shooting activity, soldiers spent one-half day in shooting and one-half day on "pit" duty. Teams of soldiers on "pit duty" raised the racks with the large bull's-eye targets, lowered the targets to mark shots with white and black round markers, raised the targets so shooters and scorers could see where their shots hit the targets, lowered and repaired targets by pasting covers over bullet holes, and raised targets for the next round of firing. The "pit duty" was non-stop action to keep fresh targets ready for the next round of shooting.

Those on pit duty were protected by the concrete structure, but could hear the hundreds of rounds cracking through the targets just a few feet overhead.

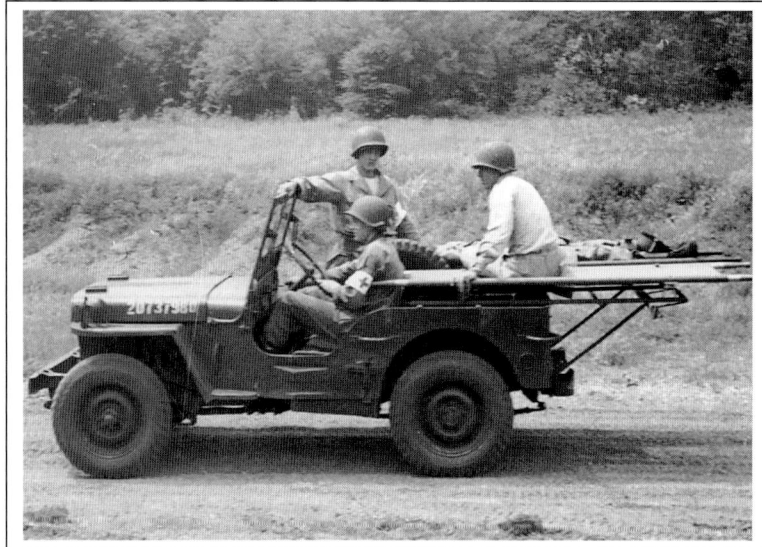

An Army doctor and two "Medics" ride toward a field Rifle Range Aid Station in a makeshift ambulance—a standard Jeep that was modified by adding a small metal extension to support two canvas litters.

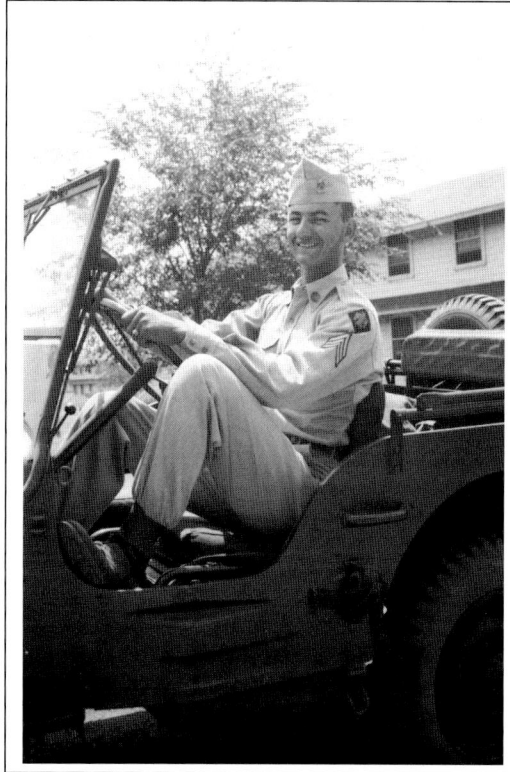

Newly-promoted "Buck Sergeant,"
Oliver in a Jeep at Fort Sill,
Oklahoma

— August 1948

Chapter Nine

Courtship and Marriage —

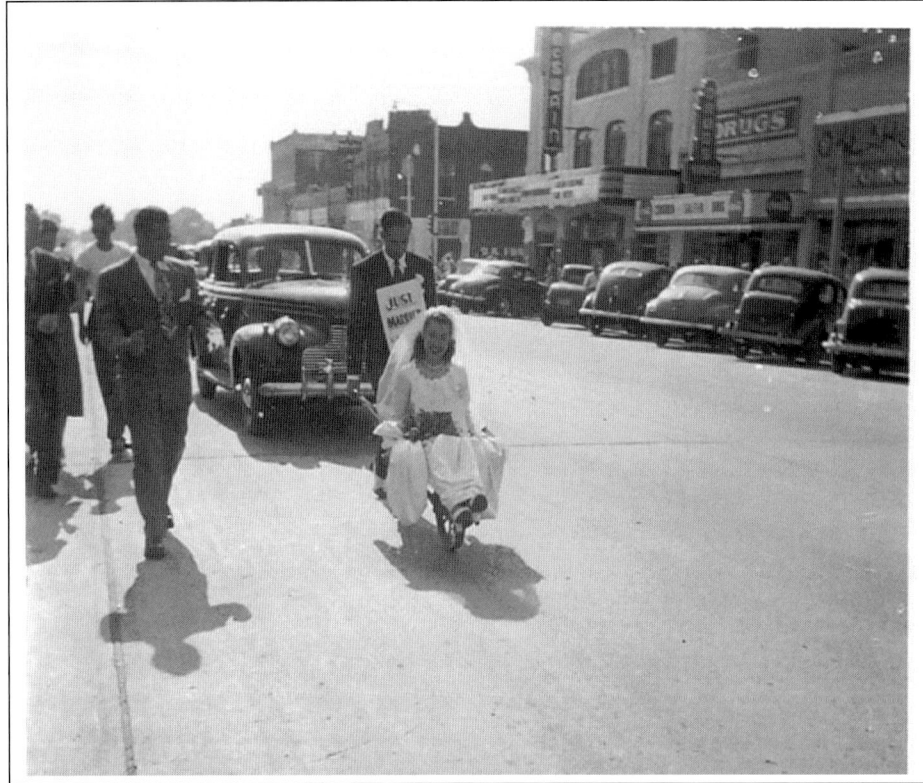

The Wheelbarrow Ride —
Groom J.B. Badgett gives his new bride, Maxine, a ride along Main Street in Ada, Oklahoma.
— June 7, 1949

Wedding Bells Are Breaking Up That Old Gang of Mine

Not a soul down on the corner,
That's a pretty certain sign,
That wedding bells are breaking up that old gang of mine.
All the boys are singing love songs,
They forgot "Sweet Adeline,"
Those wedding bells are breaking up that old gang of mine.
There goes Jack, there goes Jim,
Down to lover's lane.
Now and then we meet again,
But they don't seem the same.
Gee, I get a lonesome feeling,
When I hear the church bells chime,
Those wedding bells are breaking up that old gang of mine.

"Wedding Bells Are Breaking Up (That Old Gang Of Mine)" is a popular barbershop quartet song that laments the loss of childhood friendships when growing up into adulthood.

Music by Sammy Fain and lyrics by Irving Kahal and Willie Raskin.
The song was published in 1929.

The marriage of Maxine Rae Kemp and James Bradley Badgett was the first wedding for the close-knit group of young people in "The Gang," many whom were members of the wedding party. The ceremony was conducted on June 7, 1949, at Oak Avenue Baptist Church, with the Rev. Chester Mason, pastor, performing the service—the beginning of the "break-up" of the special group of young people.

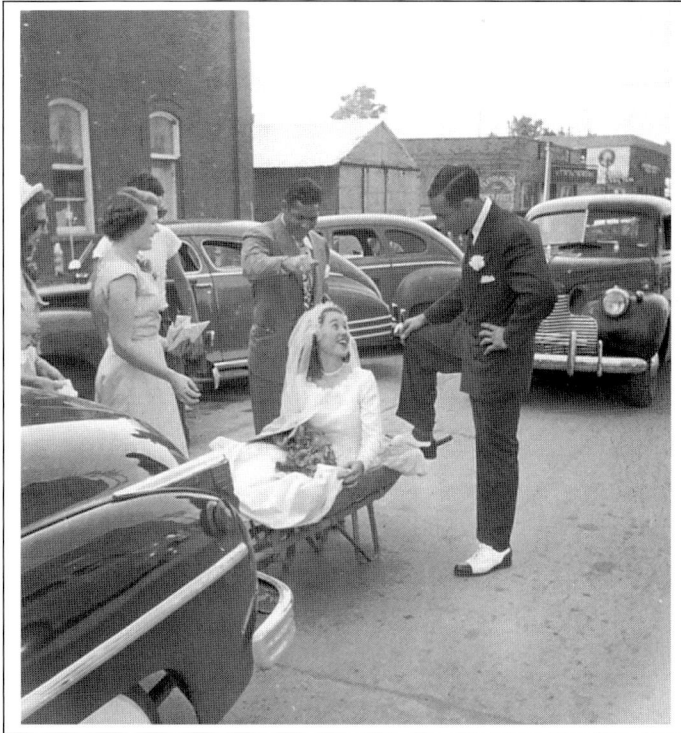

Ready to Go —
J.B. Badgett and his new bride,
Maxine, prepare for a Saturday
afternoon wheelbarrow ride
down Main Street of Ada,
Oklahoma, as friends sprinkle
rice on the bride,

Young men in the wedding party
simply stopped busy traffic and
the newlyweds made a short trip
through the business district,
cheered by shoppers and by-
standers who didn't seem to be
the least bit upset with the
unusual activity.

The Wheelbarrow Ride and Other Wedding Traditions —

Wedding traditions change through the years and a variety of clamorous traditions give newlywed couples "best wishes" for their new life together. Most traditions simply require the bride and groom to be good sports as friends and neighbors have fun at the expense of the newlyweds.

Transporting a bride home in a wheelbarrow pushed by the groom was a tradition that may have roots in western European practices. Sometimes, the groom gave the bride a ride in a wheelbarrow around the block on which the church or other wedding site was located. For the first wedding of any of special group of Ada friends, "the Gang" took the tradition to a higher level—a ride along the city's Main Street on a Saturday afternoon, the busiest day of the week—without permission from anyone. In those unique days, though, no one seemed concerned. Police, business owners and downtown shoppers simply joined in the fun with applause and cheers.

Other wedding traditions also were in place. Tying old shoes and tin cans to the back of the couple's car apparently stems from Tudor times when guests would throw shoes at the bride and groom, with great luck being bestowed on them if they or their carriage were hit. In Anglo Saxon times the groom to establish his authority symbolically struck the bride with a shoe. Brides would then throw shoes at their bridesmaids to see who would marry next.

The tin cans tied to the bumper and the honking of horns in a caravan of cars following the "escaping" newlyweds are seen as part of the Middle Ages wedding tradition of banging pots, ringing cowbells and generally making a lot of disturbing noise after the marriage ceremony in order to ward off evil spirits.

The practice of staging a Shivaree was more common in rural areas but began to fade away in the cities and towns. The Shivaree was a clamorous salutation made to a newlywed couple—often conducted in the middle of the night with the party of friends and neighbors sneaking up on the couple's home or honeymoon, then wake the couple and cause them to come outside to see what was going on. The assembled party would then wish them a blissful marriage, and the couple would be obligated to serve snacks and liquid refreshments to the gathered throng.

Dating couples began planning marriages. Betty See and Oren Pursley, on left, and Maxine Kemp and J. B. Badget, on right, were the first couples of "The Gang" to announce engagements. Vinita Shirley, center, and Clarence Oliver were engaged a few months later.

Small group parties in family homes, such as this party in the See's home. were regular events. Light refreshments, games, listening to records—and just conversation—were enjoyed.

Betty See and Oren Pursley (at right) were one of the first couples to announce engagement plans. Mary Nell Turley is pictured at the left.

— Fall 1948

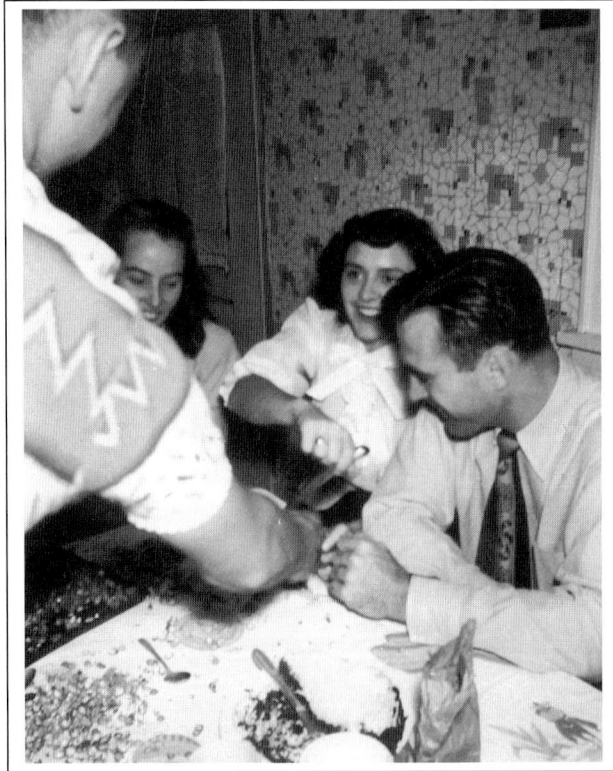

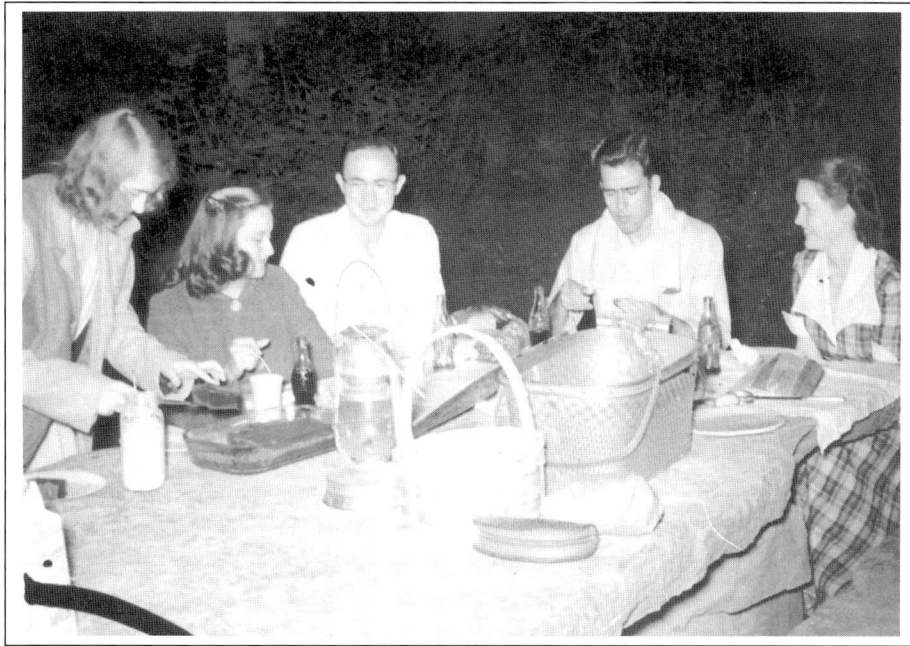

The "just friends" group of young people started to become "couples" as friendships turned to dating and then to "going steady." Vinita Shirley, Betty Mitchell, Ed Haley, Giles Mitchell and Betty Sturdevant are pictured on a nighttime picnic in Wintersmith Park. A kerosene lantern provided light for the event.

— Fall 1949

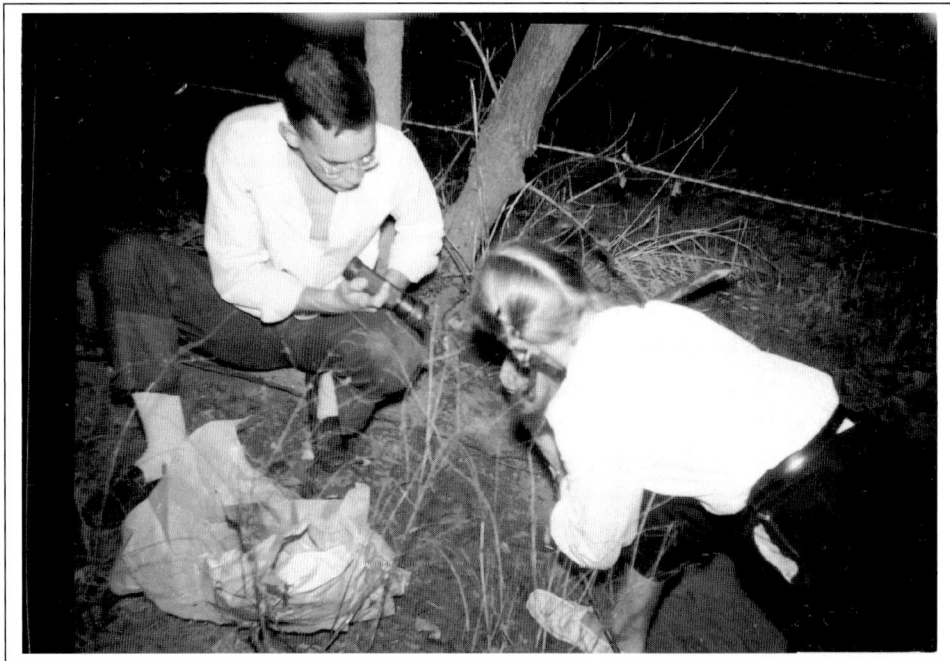

Ben Floyd and Billie Jean Fathree on a "snipe hunt" date.
— Fall 1948

The Snipe Hunt —

A snipe hunt was a practical joke, a form of "wild-goose chase," that involved experienced people making fun of gullible newcomers by giving them an impossible task—the search for a bird called the "snipe"— with the search involving a preposterous method of catching it, such as running around the woods carrying a bag or making strange noises.

Since the supposed snipe didn't exist, the hunt never succeeded, no matter how foolishly the newcomer acted. To extend the joke, there actually is a species of bird called a snipe. The success of the joke depended in part on the victim's ignorance of this, as the snipe is found primarily in wetlands and the joke is invariably played in wooded areas.

In truth, most teenagers who willingly went on a "snipe hunt" while on a double date knew this was a practical joke, but a fun way to spend some time together, walking around the woods on a nice fall evening with a full moon overhead, and pretending to "call the snipes" — another example of a "time of innocence."

Vinita Shirley and Clarence Oliver were pulled to the front at the BSU Sweetheart Banquet when friends at the East Central College Baptist Student Union learned that Vinita had received an "engagement ring" earlier that evening. The newly engaged couple joined Mr. and Mrs. Hoipkemier, who were being honored on their 50th Wedding Anniversary.

— February 14, 1950

Bob Bartlett and Wanda Graves joined the "engaged" to be married group in 1950. They married the next year.

— Fall 1949

The beautiful Platt National Park near Sulphur, Oklahoma, was a favorite place for restful outings, picnics, swimming and viewing the scenery. Vinita Shirley is pictured on top Bromide Hill, the highest point in the Park. Vinita and Clarence returned to the park on their Honeymoon in August 1950, and revisited this identical location on their 50th wedding anniversary, August 7, 2000.

— Summer 1949

Vinita June Shirley wading in Pennington Creek at Devil's Den Park on a summer Sunday afternoon.

Making Plans —

Vinita, sitting in the living room of her soon-to-be "in-laws," studied a book about weddings in preparation for a planned fall wedding.

Those plans were changed when the Korean War began in June 1950, forcing the couple to move the wedding date to early August.
— Spring 1950

Young College students, Vinita Shirley and Clarence Oliver, were "going steady" in 1949. Vinita's pet dog, a Cocker spaniel named "Smokey," rested on top the Oliver family car, a 1938 Chevrolet sedan, in front of the Shirley's home on West 12th Street, Ada, Oklahoma. Russell's Grocery and Market, a neighborhood "Mom and Pop" grocery store, was located next door to the family residence.
— Spring 1949

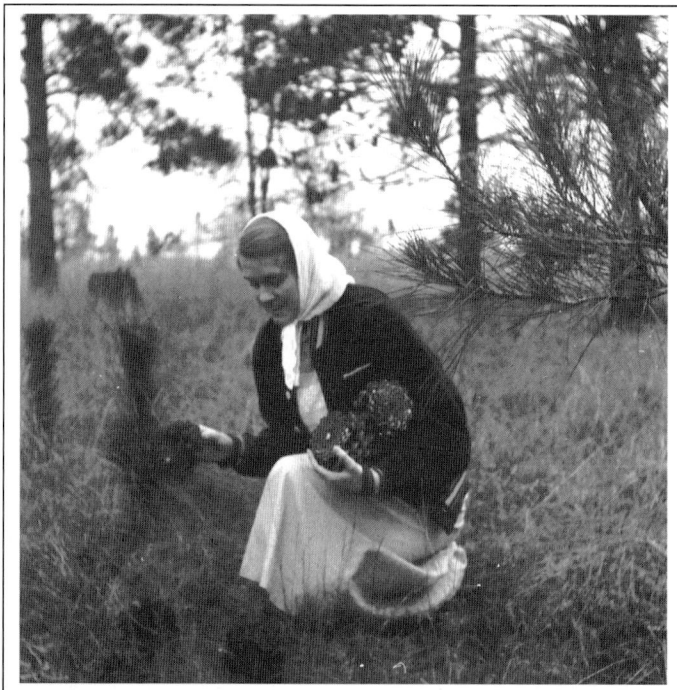

Vinita loved to gather pinecones on a Sunday afternoon in the pine forests near DeRidder, Louisiana, the new home of the newlywed Vinita and Clarence Oliver.

The huge pinecones seemed very unusual for an Oklahoma girl.
— Fall 1950

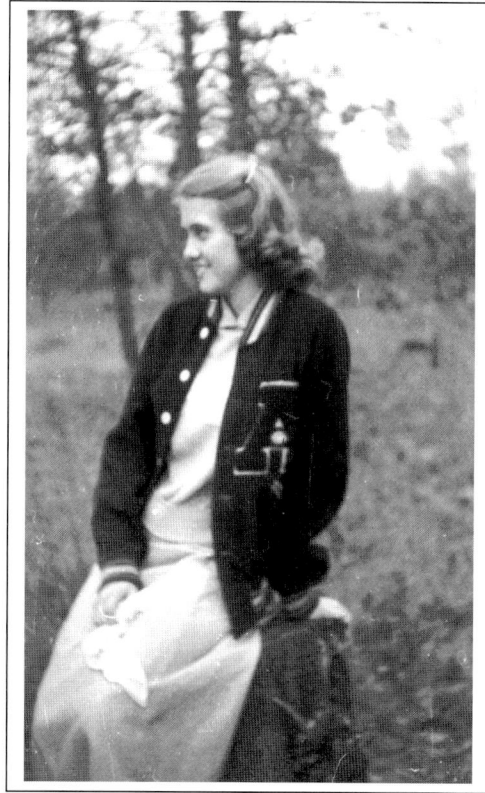

A young bride far from home—
Vinita, wearing Clarence's high school
letterman's jacket, on a Sunday afternoon
near DeRidder, Louisiana,
　　　　　　　　　— Fall 1950

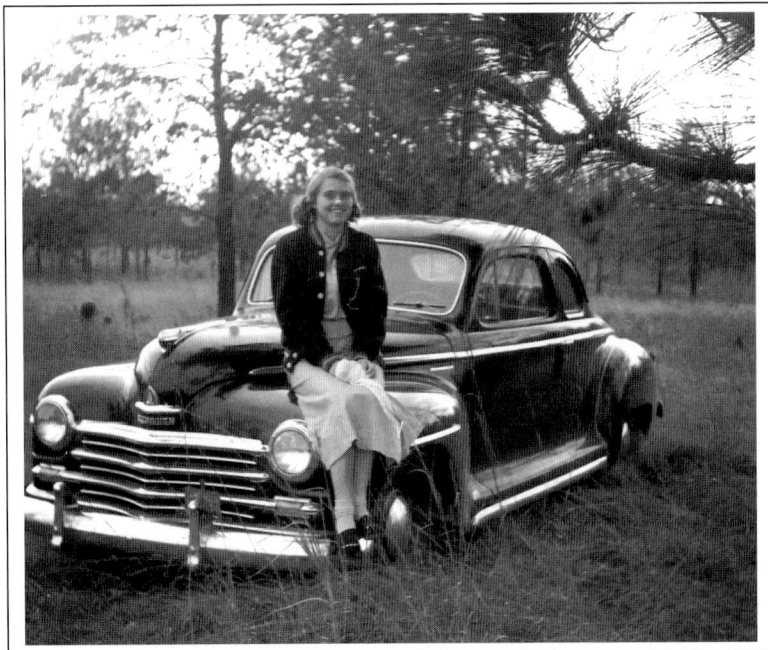

Vinita sitting on the fender of the Olivers' first car, a 1948 Plymouth coupe, on a Sunday afternoon near DeRidder, Louisiana
— Fall 1950

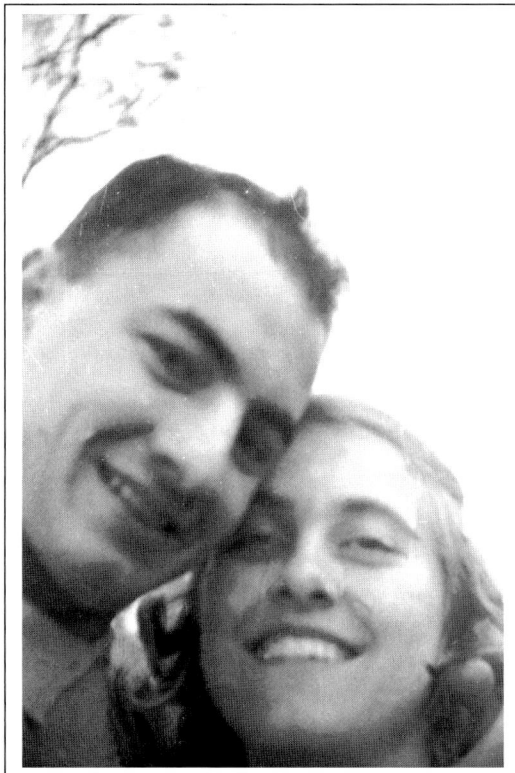

Newlyweds—Clarence and Vinita

Self-portrait.
Camera at arm's length.
— 1950

The Shell-Seeker—Vinita gathers shells that washed up on the Gulf of Mexico beach, near Port Arthur, Texas

— Winter 1950

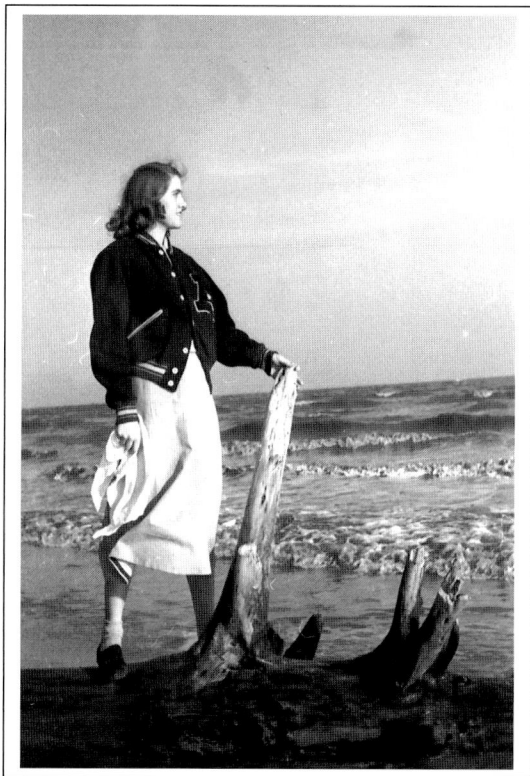

Vinita on driftwood log on Gulf of Mexico beach near Port Arthur, Texas.
   — Early Winter 1950

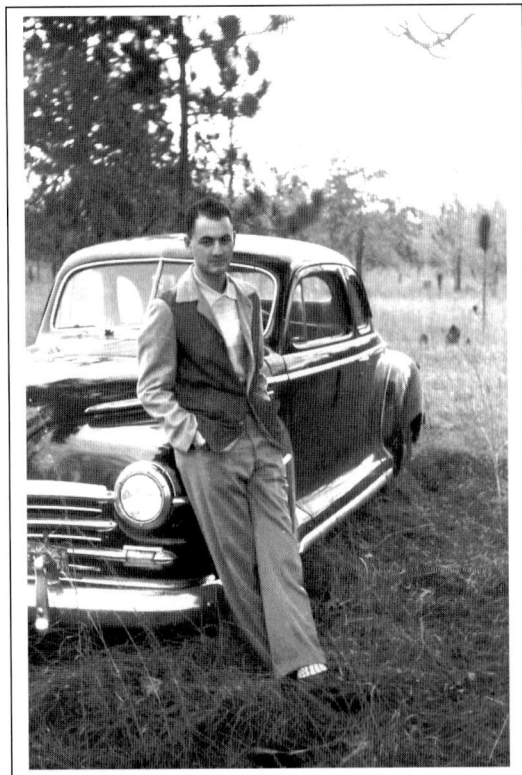

Clarence Oliver, on a Sunday afternoon, near DeRidder, Louisiana.
              — Fall 1950

Chapter Ten

The Cameras —

The Cameras —

  Clarence Oliver principally used four different personal cameras during the years of 1945 to 1950 as he honed his skills as a photographer. Photographs shown in this book are from negatives "snapped" using all four cameras.

  Photos and brief information about each of the cameras used by Oliver are shown on the following pages.

Kodak No. 2 Folding Autographic
120 mm Roll Film Camera

A Kodak No. 2 Folding Autographic Brownie Camera, purchased by Oliver's parents, Clarence, Sr., and Jewel Oliver, near the time of their marriage in 1927, was an early-day favorite camera used by Oliver. The camera had an imitation leather cover, folding bellows, reversible reflecting viewfinder, sliding focus with lock, and used 120mm roll film. The picture size was 2-1/5 inches by 3-1/4 inches.

The camera had a Kodak f/7.9 lens and a Kodak shutter with four settings, "T" for time exposures, "B" for "bulb" or very short time exposures, and "25 and 50" speed settings. The lens had five stop openings, from 4 to 64 diaphragm settings. The shutter was snapped using a pushpin cable release or by touching a shutter lever mounted on top the shutter.

A small, narrow spring door on the back of the camera permitted the photographer to autograph the photo or write information using a small metal stylus. Thus. the word, "Autographic," in the camera's name. An automatic safety spring border pressed paper into contact with the back of the film, and the impression of the stylus left an image of the writing on the film. The writing appeared in white when the negative was developed.

In 1948, a small pinhole occurred in the folding bellows, permitting light to leak into the bellows and causing a small shadow on some negatives. Oliver was unable to find the exact spot of the pinhole. The repair was never made.

Kodak No. 2 Folding Autographic Camera

Ansco Clipper
616 mm Roll Film Camera

Ansco Clipper
Fixed focus lens, single speed,
616 mm roll film camera

The Ansco Clipper was a simple "point and shoot" camera made by Agfa-Ansco and Ansco from the 1930s into the 1950s. The camera permitted the photographer to take 15 images on 616 mm roll film, with 2x2½ inches negative size.

Oliver purchased a new Ansco Camera in 1945 in Ada, Oklahoma, at a drug store where he worked at a part time sales clerk and also as a "soda jerk" at the drug store fountain. He found that the single speed shutter often resulted in some "blurred" images at parades and sporting events where subject were moving.

The Ansco camera had metal retractable bellows. The lens board pulled out of the camera body for taking pictures, and collapsed to make the camera more compact when not in use. The focus and aperture were fixed, while the shutter had two settings, "I" for instant and "B" for "bulb" or very short time exposures. A metal rod on the top of the bellows was pulled out to initiate the "bulb" mode. A small, round viewfinder was on top the camera case.

Ansco Camera Company, located in Binghamton, New York, was originally formed as Anthony & Scovill in 1902. The name was shortened to Ansco in 1907.

Argus C3
35 mm Cartridge Roll Film Camera

The Argus C3 was a low priced rangefinder camera produced from 1939 to 1966 in Michigan. Photographers commonly referred to the camera as "The Brick," due to its shape, size and weight. Oliver acquired a used Argus C3 in 1948 through a trade-purchase from a college friend.

The C3 was constructed primarily of Bakelite plastic and metal castings. The design featured an unusual and simplistic diaphragm shutter built into the camera body, so that the camera could make use of interchangeable lenses without the need for a complex focal plane shutter. The rangefinder utilized a separate viewfinder from that of the regular viewfinder and was coupled to the lens through a series of gears located on the outside of the camera body. The profusion of knobs, gears, buttons, levers, and dials on the camera lent it a very "scientific" look that was found to be one of the things buyers most liked about the camera in customer surveys.

It has been argued the Argus C3 is responsible for popularizing the use of 35mm film, and considering the long production run and the number of Argus C3 cameras made, this may very well be true especially in the United States.

Argus C3 — "The Brick"
35 mm Cartridge Roll Film Camera

Pre-Anniversary Speech Graphic 3¼ x 4¼-inch Sheet Film Camera, with focal plane shutter.

The Speed Graphic is commonly called the most famous press camera. The cameras were produced by the Graflex Company in Rochester, New York. The first Speed Graphic cameras were produced in 1912 and various improved models continued until 1973. The Speed Graphic was standard equipment for many American press photographers until the mid-1960s.

Oliver bought a used Pre-Anniversary Speed Graphic at a Camera store in Stillwater, Oklahoma, in early 1950 while he was a student at Oklahoma A&M College, with the intent to use the camera in his planned work as a free-lance photographer.

The authentic Speed Graphic has a focal plane shutter that the Crown Graphic and Century Graphic models do not possess. The focal plane shutter (a back shutter located in front of the sheet film holder) permits shutter settings up to 1/1000th of a second, valuable for high-speed sports photography.

The Speed Graphic was a slow camera, though. Each exposure required the photographer to change the film sheet, focus the camera, cock the shutter, and press the shutter. Faster shooting could be achieved with the Grafmatic film holder, a six sheet film "changer" that held each sheet in a septum.

Photographers had to be conservative and anticipate when the action was about to take place to take the right picture.

Epilogue —

The lives of the people who are portrayed in this book did not end in 1950 when the Korean War began. Most enjoyed long life and successful careers

Each of us, in part, is a product of our birth and ancestry. But the influence of other people, especially close friends, such as those who were a part of "the Gang," and the many experiences, some shared and some separate from those friends, helped mold our lives.

In the final chapter of an earlier book, *One from the Least and Disappearing Generation: a Memoir of a Depression-Era Kid*, published in 2003, I wrote these words about the night of my graduation from high school:

"The ceremony was uneventful. Superintendent Rex O. Morrison told the 100-plus seniors of the challenges and opportunities, that were ahead—an oft-repeated message he had shared with graduates of other years. Principal Trice L. Broderick assisted with the awarding of diplomas.

"After receiving the empty diploma cover, which would be filled with an official diploma after the borrowed cap and gown were returned to the school office, I walked alone across the campus that had become so familiar in six years—three in Junior High School and three in High School. I don't remember particularly why, but I was alone after the graduation program concluded. I rather enjoyed the quiet walk across campus to the Senior High School to turn-in the cap and gown, providing assurance that no library fines or any other fees were still owed to the school, and to receive a diploma. I was officially a brand new High School Graduate.

"Earlier in the month, while writing in a Senior Year Memories Book in response to the printed questions about plans for the future, my response about future careers indicated that I wanted to be a newspaper editor, and if not successful in that area, to be a photographer. That night I didn't have the slightest idea if I could be or would be either an editor or photographer, neither or both. I was to become both, and much more.

"Right then, I realized that tomorrow I would be just another recent high school graduate hitting the streets looking for a job—any job—to meet the immediate needs of a young man with dreams and no resources.

"But, I do remember that these haunting words of one of the poems learned in Miss Daisy Britt's American Literature class crept into my mind: (Oliver 2003)

"The woods are lovely, dark and deep.
But I have promises to keep,
And miles to go before I sleep,
And miles to go before I sleep."

The naïve young people who grew up during those days began that long walk that Robert Frost so simply and eloquently described in his poem, *Stopping by Woods on a Snowy Evening*. (Frost 1923)

What became of them?

The strong background of moral and ethical standards that were embraced because of the shared experiences in church and school most certainly influenced all our lives, career choices, and service to others. Several of the young people became educators—classroom teachers, principals, superintendents of schools, university professors, and university administrators. During a time when "stay-at-home" mother was an admired status, several of the ladies were homemakers who nurtured their families and also contributed many years of service in church and community projects. At least three enjoyed lifelong careers as military officers—in the United States Army, the United States Air Force and the United States Navy. There was a meteorologist and a journalist. Several became enterprising business leaders, highly successful in different fields, some acquiring significant wealth. The lives of a few were interrupted by untimely deaths.

As individuals and as a group, they contributed greatly to society in general and to their communities in particular.

The young people whose lives are pictured and discussed in this book are of the generation whose early childhood was lived during the nation's worst ever time of massive economic difficulties—the Great Depression. That difficult time was followed immediately by a worldwide war that impacted every family in the land, left indelible impressions, which, even in adulthood, affected the beliefs and behaviors of those who lived through those years.

But, strengthened by those experiences, the young people of that era became leaders during the decades that followed and as they moved from a life before television, before FM radios, before computers and cellular telephones they became one of the most "savvy" of generations.

All in all, the youth from the days of "peace" and "innocence" did rather well with their lives.

Acknowledgments—

There are so many people who have provided encouragement and assistance to me during the days of research and writing of this book that I most certainly will overlook someone and fail to give proper acknowledgment to all who deserve my words of appreciation.

For any such unintentional oversight, I sincerely apologize.

I gratefully acknowledge these special people:

Prior to her death in October 2009, my wife, Vinita, who has been the love of my life since she was 15 years old, was a wonderful encourager. During the days when draft chapters of the photos and text were still in "rough" form, she loved to look at the photographs and recall those days so long ago that were from that "time of peace, season of innocence." My regret is that she did not live to see the finished work. This book is lovingly offered "in her memory."

The initial suggestion that I begin this effort came from our son, Paul A. Oliver, and his lovely wife, Kathy, who recalled all the photographs that were taken during the days of my youth and who encouraged me to assemble those photographs and stories into a special book that would tell of a unique era in our country's history—so that our children, grandchildren, great-grandchildren and future generations might know about a time that really existed but for present generations seems almost like a "fairy tale."

Our daughter, Shirley J. Parsons, and our son, Mark G. Oliver, and their spouses, were quick to endorse the idea for the book and eagerly reviewed bits and pieces of draft chapters, showed great interest in the photographs and the story, always providing encouraging words when so many challenges arose that temporarily disrupted the work. I am grateful to all of them.

A special friend, Brigadier General Gerald Wright, former Air Force jet fighter pilot, retired commander of the Oklahoma Air National Guard, retired Oklahoma State Senator, and a long-time friend who seems almost like a "younger brother," provided almost weekly encouragement and persistently urged me to "keep on" with the work.

Several friends from those memorable high school and college days who were willing to offer assistance and constructive critique of this effort are held in particular esteem. Billie Jean (Fathree) Floyd, a friend of many decades, a former Oklahoma State Senator and a Professor at East Central University in Ada, Oklahoma, greatly assisted by confirming identity of people in photos—as well as reviewing and critiquing draft chapters from an unusual perspective of having lived many of the experiences told in the book. She and her late husband, Ben C. Floyd, were among my "best friends" during those days of our youth—and for all the years afterwards. Professor Floyd also led me to a great resource friend, Ann Klepper. M.D., a physician and author, whose book, *The Ada Rodeo: an Incredible Saga*, tells a unique story of a special time in the community. Dr. Klepper's research and writings helped to confirm dates and better explain the history of the "Rodeo Days" that many of us experienced in my hometown in the days of our youth.

Praise also goes to Lavelle Sanders of Bentonville, Arkansas, for helping insure greater accuracy in the book by his sharp memory of specific events and people—as well as for his words of encouragement. Similar appreciation is extended to Ed C. Haley, Jr., of Lehigh Acres, Florida, another friend from those high school and college days, a career U. S. Navy Petty Officer, and one-time college roommate at Oklahoma A&M College, for his willingness to review photographs and to assist in confirming names and events.

A special expression of gratitude goes to Barbara (Brown) Kimbrough of Broken Arrow, Oklahoma, a historian in her own right and daughter of a historian, for her appreciation of the project and for her regular admonishments, made in person and via email messages, to "keep on writing." There were days when those messages caused me to return to the task when I was tempted to postpone the effort to another day.

I am indebted to Adam J. Foreman of Broken Arrow, Oklahoma, one of the most talented of graphic artists, for his valuable aid in transforming my draft ideas into such an impressive and inviting book cover. He is known for his volunteerism and his *Pro bono publico* efforts in promoting many Broken Arrow community groups and events, especially for his work with the Broken Arrow Arts and Humanities Council. I am grateful for his assistance

For all the others who inquired about progress and expressed encouraging words through the many months when this has been "a work in progress," I also express my appreciation. All of you are wonderful, gracious friends. I struggle with how to express appreciation for all the support. The two small words, "Thank You," seem so inadequate; but, until I can find better words, these are written to each of you with sincere gratitude.

Clarence G. Oliver, Jr.
Broken Arrow, Oklahoma
— 2011

278

References—

Books

Frost, Robert. (1923). Stopping by woods on a snowy evening. In Lathem, Edward C. (Ed.), *The poetry of Robert Frost* (pp. 224-225). (1969). Holt, Rinehart and Winston, New York, New York.

Irving, Washington. (1886). *A Tour of the Prairies,* John B. Alden, New York, New York.

Klepper, Ann, M.D. (2009). *The Ada rodeo: an incredible saga*. PAST Foundation, Inc., Author House Publishing, Bloomington, Indiana.

Krocker, Marvin E. & Logsdon, Guy W. (1998). *Ada, Oklahoma: queen city of the Chickasaw nation*. Ada Chamber of Commerce, Donning Company Publishers, Virginia Beach, Virginia.

Oliver, Clarence G., Jr. (2003) *One from the least and disappearing generation: a memoir of a depression-era kid*, Trafford Publishing, Vancover, British Columbia, Canada.

Newspapers and Other Publications

Ada Evening News (1945 to 1950), selected issues; August 7, 1945, p1; August 16, 1945, p1; September 2, 1945, p1; April 14, 1947, p1; January 30, 1948, p 8; April 25, 1948, Sec. 2, p1; July 19, 1948, p1; August 8, 1948, Sec.2, p1; January 26, 1949, p1; May 8, 1949, p 2; August 9, 1949, p1; June 24, 1950, p1; and July 2, 1950, p1, The News Publishing Company, Ada, Oklahoma. Used with permission from The Ada Evening News. © 1945, 1946, 1947, 1948, 1949, 1950, 2010. The News Publishing Company.

Seattle Post-Intelligencer (August 15, 1945, p1.). Seattle, Washington. Hearst Corporation, New York, New York. Used with permission from the Hearst Corporation. © 1945, 2010, Hearst Corporation.

Stars and Stripes (August 15, 1945, p1.). Stars and Stripes, Washington, D.C. Used with permission from Stars and Stripes. © 1945, 2010, Stars and Stripes.

"Wedding Bells Are Breaking Up That Old Gang of Mine." (1929). Music by Sammy Fain, lyrics by Irving Kahal and Willie Raskin.

Index

A

B

C

D

F

284